Peter Melvin Wege 1920-2014

The History of The Wege Foundation:
and the Man Behind It

Copyright © The Wege Foundation
All Rights Reserved.
Published in the United States
Printed in the United States of America
Author and Editor *Susan Brace Lovell*
Book designed by *Brad Hineline*
ISBN 978-0-692-08152-5

INTRODUCTION

"This History enables present and future generations to learn and respect all that Peter Wege did in his lifetime to address a wide range of problems, conditions, and situations all of which will have an impact on the future. His contributions were not only in Grand Rapids, Ann Arbor, and the state of Michigan, but literally throughout the world."

Jonathan W. Bulkley - Peter M. Wege Endowed Professor Emeritus of Sustainable Systems, Professor Emeritus of Resources Policy, School of Natural Resources & Environment and Professor Emeritus of Civil & Environmental Engineering, College of Engineering.

ELLEN SATTERLEE IN 2011

When she heard the total of Wege's giving to Grand Rapids Art Museum of over $60 million, Ellen Satterlee's response was immediate: "It is overwhelming when you see how very generous PMW has been over the years. For a long time I have said that I was probably the only one who really had any idea because I saw both sides—Foundation and personal. I don't even think he realizes the extent because he really doesn't keep track—he just does the next right thing. But for over fifty years of generosity between his personal giving and the Wege Foundation's grants, it's always been about the mission—never about the man.

"Over that half century, few good causes have not felt Peter's helping hand. Whether we're talking about the environment, the arts, health care, or easing human suffering, Grand Rapids is a better place to live because of Peter Wege's lifelong passion for always doing the next right thing.

"And through the years, it seems very Biblical—the more he gave away, the more he accumulated. It has truly been incredible. Some days it does seem like funny money because it is all really just paperwork from this seat. But when you look at what this community has become—well, it just wouldn't be the same without his very specific involvement."

Ellen Satterlee
Executive Assistant of The Wege Foundation 1988-1998.
Executive Director 1998-2010. President 2010-2015.

TERRI McCARTHY

Peter was a master at gathering people. They all wanted to be near him because of his "can-do" spirit. And he thought so big that he was inspirational to all of them. How could they not come! It was how he brought together all of the college sustainability leaders for years at University of Michigan and then Aquinas College and one at Michigan Tech University where we met so many awesome people that he ended up funding.

And then he funded the Island School in the Bahamas because Chris Maxey was so cool, a former Navy SEAL. Peter loved that. If Peter saw a "star," he went outside the guidelines and that was what was so exciting. And, of course, Dan Janzen is the best example, so far away but too "Einstein" not to fund.

And the Muskegon River Watershed Project wouldn't have happened without Peter's affection for Jack Bails! Jack Bails called Peter his "soul mate." When they met, it was the beginning of so much. The first person he called when getting the group together for the Great Lakes HOW Coalition was Jack Bails. Jack had to be part of the team!

This book makes me so happy and sad at the same time. A man we loved so much, I can't imagine I'll ever meet another spirit like his in my lifetime.

Terri McCarthy
1998-2004 Wege Foundation Program Officer;
2004-2014 Vice President of Programs.

AQUINAS COLLEGE

As I entered the Center for Economicology at City High School, I had no clue what Economicology was, who Peter Wege was, or why it was important. Memorizing the 6 E's: Economics, Ecology, Environment, Empathy, Ethics, and Education, I began to see how economics correlates with ecology, and how both of them correlate to ethics, empathy, education, and the environment. This theme of interconnectedness gave me a true sense of how important sustainability is.

In the fall of 2003 Aquinas College unveiled the nation's first ever Sustainable Business program as the result of great work by Peter Wege, The Wege Foundation, and some visionary leaders at Aquinas. Having gone through Peter Wege's programs from 6th grade through graduate school, I feel very fortunate and quite ready to tackle the future.

Dylan Hall
2016 Aquinas College graduate with a Bachelor of Science in Sustainable Business.

AUTHOR'S NOTE

In late 1989 I got a phone call from a kind voice saying she was Ellen Satterlee and that "Mr. Wege would like to meet with you." Ellen explained that he needed a writer and knew my name as the editor of Cadence Newspaper at the time. Soon after, we three gathered in The Wege Foundation's newly renovated upstairs office on the corner of South Division and Wealthy.

For Peter, the space was almost sacred. It had been his father's apartment when Peter Martin Wege moved to Grand Rapids to start Metal Office Furniture in 1912. It was where Peter's dad brought his bride to live in 1917 and it was Peter's first home after he was born in 1920. To know Peter Wege was to know he revered the parents he referred to as "my genius father" and "my sainted mother," Sophia Louise Dubridge.

But I knew none of the family history that day as Peter brought out several thick yellow legal pads filled with penciled handwriting. And it didn't matter. I was already intrigued. Scanning the first page, I knew two things. He was a big thinker who wrote in even bigger terms. I knew what he needed. Simplifying. Clarifying. Specifying. Cutting redundancies.

Then, after moving The Wege Foundation office into his house and before I knew it, he was sending me home with canvas bags full of environmental books. He'd progressed beyond ruminations. He wanted our writer/editor partnership to produce a book on "economicology," a word he coined to advocate for humanity's obligation to balance the needs of the economy with those of the ecology.

"We have to use all these quotes, Susan," he'd say handing me a book to leaf through. The problem was he'd pretty much yellow-highlighted lengthy chunks of text on every page!

It was so Peter. He wanted everyone to know all that he'd learned from these visionary environmentalists. That meant we had to quote *all* the writers in *all* their wisdom. Fortunately Peter was also always willing to listen. He accepted that we couldn't just do a book of other people's quotes. It had to be Peter's book drawing on his favorite environmental writers to support his thesis of economicology. That was the beginning of what turned out to be a twenty-plus year partnership and friendship.

In the end ECONOMICOLOGY was published in 1998 followed by ECONOMICOLOGY II. And they were both Peter's books replete with quotes and summaries from the best of the best thinkers in the environmental world.

From that first day on South Division with the legal pads, I was Peter's "word" person. And I was privileged to become part of what we called "Team Wege." As I tagged along with Peter and Ellen and Terri visiting the good causes he and The Foundation supported, the old reporter couldn't help herself. I began taking notes—not even sure why at the beginning.

But the more I heard and saw and learned about Peter and The Wege Foundation's work, the more I knew why I'd been scribbling all along. And taking photographs. And interviewing folks in the non-profits The Wege Foundation supported.

The story of what Peter M. Wege and The Wege Foundation have done to make this world a better place had to be told. People needed to hear what his hallmark "doing the most good" has meant for the environment, the arts, human services, health care, and the one mission Peter said was most important and integrated into the other four: education.

This book is about the life of Peter M. Wege who funded a small library in Chase, Michigan because his friend and archivist Diane Johnson lived there and loved the library. It's about how Denny Sturtevant got him to buy the same building twice and give it away both times. It's about his insistence on dignifying the people at Heartside Ministry by building them new space.

It is the history of the family foundation he started in August 1967 that has done all the good it could for half a century and continues to do so. It is also the story of philanthropy in a city known for its generosity. It is the story of charitable collaborations. From the beginning when the W.K. Kellogg Foundation stepped up for The Wege Foundation's first mission creating the Center for Environmental Study, the good works were not done solo. Without the village of partnering foundations, individual donors, the caring souls who first saw a need and did something about it, and the dedicated people who continue to lead the non-profits, Peter M. Wege and The Wege Foundation could never have done "the most good" they have for half a century.

Grand Rapids is a better place because of The Wege Foundation —and "The Man Behind It." This is their story.

Susan Brace Lovell
August 2017

ACKNOWLEDGEMENTS

As an only child, Peter Melvin Wege was an anomaly in some ways. He turned down the vast majority of "naming" honors he was offered because his gifts were never about him. They were about the cause. The few times he acquiesced—the Peter M. Wege Aquinas Ballroom, the Grand Rapids Ballet, the Mind, Body, Spirit wing of Saint Mary's Hospital—he made one thing clear. "That is the name of my father and it is for him too."

But his style of giving, both personally and through The Wege Foundation, was also atypical for someone raised by adoring parents who never thought they'd have children. Peter Wege was all about collaboration. Teamwork. Partnerships. Indeed, he loved challenge grants and was known for luring in other givers by offering to match whatever they gave.

The word was out in the non-profit community that if you had a new or small or unfamiliar cause, The Wege Foundation was the place to start. Peter had a heart for people who dreamed of doing something good that hadn't been done before. And he didn't need pages of backup data. If he believed in the person asking for support, that was good enough. And once Peter and The Wege Foundation were on board, these new startups had the credibility to bring in other donors.

This book carries on Peter M. Wege's legacy of collaboration. The people named here, all friends of Peter's, all busy, took the time to read the manuscript. How important their help has been! Their various additions, corrections, suggestions, and comments have been woven into the fabric of this story. To a person they were eager to contribute out of their fondness and respect for "The Man Behind" The Wege Foundation.

Sister Aquinas Weber
LeeAnn Arkema
Melanie Bielen
Bert Bleke
Jonathan Bulkley
Elizabeth Crouch
Carol Dirkse
Dana Friis-Hansen
George Heartwell
Dale Hovenkamp
Gregory A. Keoleian
Terri McCarthy
Phil McCorkle
Jody Price
Father Mark Przybysz
Julie Ridenour
Ellen Satterlee
Denny Sturtevant
Mark Van Putten
John Varineau

Peter Melvin Wege 1920-2014

Peter Melvin Wege 1920-2014

THE HISTORY OF THE WEGE FOUNDATION: AND THE MAN BEHIND IT

A HALF—CENTURY DOING "ALL THE GOOD YOU CAN"
1967-2017

CHAPTER ONE

HOW IT ALL BEGAN

"Make sure your giving is from
the heart—not to make an impression."

Peter Wege, December 9, 2004

The history of The Wege Foundation legally created on July 12, 1967, cannot be written without telling the story of the man behind it. To understand The Wege Foundation's mission is to understand the vision and passion of its founder, Peter Martin Wege. And from the first grants on, Peter Melvin made it clear that the reason The Foundation had the resources to make the world better was thanks to the genius of his father, Peter Martin Wege.

In 1911 at age 41, Peter Martin Wege, an experienced sheet-metal worker with an inventive mind, moved from Marietta, Ohio, to work for the Macey Company in Grand Rapids. The company had recruited Wege to build the metal support structures for the rollers under the drawers of Macey's wooden file cabinets. Wege, however, had his own dream of manufacturing metal furniture himself. With his legally registered patents for improved file drawers, steel wastebaskets, and safes, in 1912 Peter M. Wege borrowed $75,000 to found Metal Office Furniture.

That investment evolved into Steelcase, Incorporated, destined to become the largest office-furniture manufacturer in the world with sales of $111 million in 1970 and over $1 billion by 1985. In 2014, the year Peter M. Wege died, sales had climbed to $2.988 billion.

In 1916, Peter Martin met pretty blue-eyed Sophia Dubridge at Macey's where she kept the books and where the new president of Metal Office Furniture was doing business. Sophia Louise Dubridge was born December 8, 1884, into a fun-loving Catholic family on the west side of Grand Rapids. She was fourteen years younger than the attractive Peter Martin who was born September 11, 1870, in Toledo, Ohio, where his German-born parents had settled.

In 1917 Peter Martin and Sophia Louise Dubridge were married in St. Andrews Church at a side altar as Wege was not a baptized Catholic. Peter Martin likely doubted he'd ever be a father as he was 47 when he married the 33-year old Sophia Louise, always 'Lou' to him. One can only imagine this entrepreneur's pride three years later when the Weges brought their son Peter Melvin, born February 19, 1920, home to apartment Three at 359 South Division where Peter Martin had lived since moving to Grand Rapids.

But even though Peter lived there only as a baby, he never forgot about his first home. Sixty years later it was a major reason behind The Wege Foundation's restoration of the deteriorating Wealthy-Division neighborhood. And Peter's first project was renovating the apartment building on the corner.

In August of 1920, the Wege family moved into their first house,

Sophia Louise and Peter Martin Wege reading a letter from their son during World War II when First Lieutenant Peter M. Wege was an Army Air Corps pilot stationed in North Africa.

a former cornfield, at 2630 Lake Drive in East Grand Rapids. When Peter Martin Wege died of mouth cancer in 1947, his son moved his own growing family into the Lake Drive home and built an attached apartment for his mother above the garage. Sophia Louise lived there until shortly before she died enjoying the company of her grandchildren.

Peter M. Wege's parents shaped the generous spirit of their only child. What had mattered to Peter Martin and Sophia Wege, who was 'Lou Lou' to her friends, would matter to their son. Their causes would become his—first in personal giving and later through The Wege Foundation. Sophia Wege, whom Peter referred to as "my sainted mother," gave freely of her time and resources to the Catholic Church and her son would go on to support Catholic causes all his life.

Although Peter Martin never converted, he fully supported his wife's devout Catholicism. He was the one who drove young Peter to school at St. Stephen's every morning getting him there in time for Mass. Nothing less than taking his only child to school would have kept Peter Martin Wege from arriving at his plant earlier than anyone else.

Peter Martin had inherited the powerful work ethic of his German ancestors, a character trait that contributed to the astronomical success of Metal Office Furniture. But it was his genius for technical improvements in molding metal into wastebaskets and safes and file cabinets that catapulted MOF ahead of the competition.

The resourceful entrepreneur drew on his years working sheet metal himself to devise new ways of shaping it into practical pieces of office furniture. His own factory experience enabled him to find and train the best metal craftsmen around.

Yet one of the most important factors in Metal Office Furniture's success was how Peter Martin Wege treated his employees. Having been a plant man himself, the founder of MOF respected what his laborers did and they knew it. They responded with an affection and a loyalty that became part of MOF's identity—and later Steelcase's.

It didn't take long for the word to get around Grand Rapids that this new metal-furniture plant was a great place to work, and Wege never had to worry about finding enough good men to work in his factory. From the day he founded the company, Peter Martin Wege wanted to make a profit; but he also established a culture respecting human values that set Metal Office Furniture, and later Steelcase, apart from other manufacturers.

This son of German immigrant parents was the man who came up with the unheard-of plan to share his company's profits with employees. He also set the unusual precedent of hiring his employees' family members, a policy that continued with Steelcase. Peter Martin Wege created the culture at MOF and later Steelcase that said this manufacturer would make the best office furniture in the country, and every employee would participate in its financial success.

Clearly, Peter Melvin Wege's parents gave their son not only the asset base upon which Peter built The Wege Foundation, but they also provided the moral compass. Sophia and Peter Martin Wege passed on to their only child the spiritual dimension of respecting every person and caring for those less fortunate. Their values would influence their son's philanthropy all his life; and they continue today to guide The Wege Foundation's governing Trustees.

Here is how Peter himself explained the Foundation's history—starting with one of his classic puns:

"The Wege Foundation would not have a legacy to stand on if it were not for the genius of Peter Martin Wege who founded the Metal Office Furniture Company in 1912. MOF, as it was affectionately called, became Steelcase, Inc., on December 1, 1954. MOF's advertising department suggested renaming the company Steelcase for the recognized brand name of its office furniture.

"The extraordinary success of the newly named Steelcase gave me the opportunity to start The Wege Foundation in 1967. The Foundation was established to help fund needed public causes in the community where I was born and raised. In 1998, we made Steelcase a public company traded on the New York Stock Exchange. This move allowed the Wege Foundation to provide more major funding for needed local causes."

CHAPTER TWO

THE EARLY GIFTS POINT TOWARD THE FUTURE FOUNDATION

"TO WASTE, TO DESTROY OUR NATURAL RESOURCES…WILL RESULT IN UNDERMINING THE DAYS OF OUR CHILDREN THE VERY PROSPERITY WHICH WE OUGHT BY RIGHT TO HAND DOWN TO THEM…"

PRESIDENT THEODORE ROOSEVELT'S MESSAGE TO CONGRESS 1907.

Nineteen twenty, the year the Wege family moved into their first house on Lake Drive in East Grand Rapids, women won the right to vote and Prohibition outlawed alcohol. The sparsely settled village where Peter would live most of his life was like moving into the country with dirt roads.

In 1922 Peter Martin hired Herman Kiel, a 17-year-old German gardener who gave young Peter his first lessons on caring for the Earth. Peter tagged along while Herman tended to the Wege's huge lawn and garden. Years later Wege recalled, "I learned that asparagus patches last a long time, rutabagas, beets, and carrots had decidedly different tastes, and they all usually ended up in one of Mom's fabulous soups."

Both the fresh flowers Sophia Wege loved and the vegetables she cooked with came from Herman Kiel's garden. Peter remembered a girl named Ella Stair arriving to clean in her father's horse and buggy from their farm at Lake Drive and the East Beltline.

St. Stephen's grade school also helped shape the visionary philanthropist Peter Wege was to become. He later wrote about his kindergarten teacher, "Sister Mary Leonard started me the way I wish every child in the world could be started—with love, compassion, and understanding."

Indeed, one of his earliest personal grants in April 1956 harked back to his beloved teacher, Sister Leonard, when Peter Wege set up a math/chemistry scholarship at Aquinas College. Fifty-two years later, Peter Wege would still be funding Aquinas students! In 2008 he sponsored Aquinas College's first Pro-Am golf tournament at Blythefield Country Club to raise money for scholarships. Aquinas graduate and Peter's friend Greg Alksnis organized that inaugural tournament and asked to name it after Peter. Wege's customary answer was, of course, "No!"

But Alksnis wouldn't accept that. "It took me half an hour of begging and pushing," Alksnis said, "before I finally wore him down." May 19, 2008, the first annual Peter M. Wege Pro Am Tournament raised over $100,000 in scholarships for Aquinas students.

While his 1956 Aquinas grant honored the nuns who'd taught him at St. Stephen, they also reflected another side of the man who would create The Wege Foundation. A visionary is a person

Holmdene, Aquinas College's administrative and faculty building, was built in 1906 for the Edward Lowe family as Holmdene Manor. In 1911 President Theodore Roosevelt slept upstairs as a guest of the Lowes. The Dominicans bought the Lowe estate in 1945 and moved Aquinas from downtown to Holmdene, the college's first classroom and office building.

who thinks so broadly in the present that he can visualize the needs of the future. Maybe Peter Wege didn't look into a crystal ball when he dedicated his scholarship to math and science, but he might as well have.

In October 1957, just months after Peter created the math/chemistry scholarship, the world was shaken when the Soviet Union launched Sputnik, the first satellite to orbit the earth. Educators across the country immediately began requiring students to take more math and science courses. But, by then, the first winner of the Wege Scholarship was already a sophomore at Aquinas majoring in exactly those subjects.

In this first gift, as with many to come, Peter Wege memorialized his father Peter Martin Wege who had died in 1947. Directing this first Aquinas scholarship toward math and chemistry, Peter demonstrated his respect to the self-taught engineering talents of his late father.

Peter wanted to make sure another bright young person like his father had educational opportunities Peter Martin didn't have as he had to drop out of his Toledo high school at age 16 to help support his family. Peter knew his father would have been gratified that his success at MOF would one day provide for young people to have what he never did: the privilege of a four-year college education in math and science.

Without a high-school degree himself, Peter Martin Wege had mastered those engineering skills through years of hard work in the steel-fabricating plants at Marietta Safe Cabinet Company in Marietta, Ohio, J.L. & J.M. Cornell Company in Cold Spring, New York, and General Fireproofing in Youngstown, Ohio. There was never a question what Peter Melvin Wege would name his gift to Aquinas. The Peter Martin Wege Scholarship was a fitting tribute to his late father.

This early bequest set a pattern for Peter Wege's philanthropy that continued into the next century. Over and over again, he would honor his parents by naming major donations for them, singularly and together. He would also—and always—be reluctant to attach his own name to his charitable gifts.

Half a century later, Peter M. Wege would turn down the ultimate "naming" right that came with an historic $20 million donation. It was vintage Peter—all about the gift, not the giver. But that story comes later.

CHAPTER THREE

FROM THROWING JAVELINS FOR U OF M TO FLYING AIRPLANES FOR HIS COUNTRY

"STEWARDSHIP IS WHAT A MAN DOES AFTER HE SAYS, 'I BELIEVE.'" W. H. GREEVER.

ECONOMICOLOGY: THE ELEVENTH COMMANDMENT,
PETER M. WEGE.

Growing up as an only child, Peter didn't feel lonely because he was surrounded by cousins and friends—and always a family dog. In 1926, Peter Martin and Sophia bought a cottage on Lake Leelanau complete with an outhouse. Peter had great memories of swimming and fishing with his cousins Eugene and Gerard Dubridge and his best friend Gordy Varneau.

Gordy's parents Oscar and Lillian Varneau, close friends of Peter's parents, owned Wealthy Theatre where the boys spent Saturdays watching cowboy movies. Some sixty years later, when Peter Wege stepped forth to save and restore Wealthy Theatre, he was remembering the fun of those Saturday afternoons with Gordy.

Peter and Gordy Varneau remained close all their lives. One of Gordy's strengths was remembering every joke he heard breaking down Peter with laughter. Not all of Gordy's jokes were fit for mixed company—perhaps explaining why Peter laughed so hard!

Decades later when Gordy's health was failing, Peter Wege made sure his lifelong best friend had the best medical care available. Over the last years of Gordy's life, Peter called him every day. Sure, Peter wanted a joke—but he also wanted Gordy to know his best friend was thinking about him.

Over the years, the two childhood friends grew into a comedy team who used laughter to help deal with life's setbacks. But they would also spend some serious hours swapping war stories as both Peter and Gordy ended up flying planes for the Army Air Corps during World War II.

In 1934 Peter's parents sent their athletic and rambunctious 14-year-old to California's San Diego Army and Navy Academy—renamed Brown Military Academy in 1937. With a faculty made up of West Point graduates, the military academy was known as the "West Point of the West."

By the time Peter began his freshman year of military school, Metal Office Furniture had weathered the worst of the Great Depression. Nineteen thirty turned out to be the only year in the 20th Century the company—renamed Steelcase in 1954—lost money. During the Depression, the senior Wege and his partners Dave Hunting and Walter Idema struggled to keep on as many employees as possible by cutting everyone's hours.

MOF's workers were grateful for whatever job the owners had for them from washing windows to sweeping floors. And they never forgot their employers' help during the Depression when millions of Americans were unemployed.

Stationed in North Africa, First Lieutenant Peter M. Wege and his fellow officers visit the ancient ruins of Egypt. In Africa Wege was also introduced to the wildlife that later influenced his philanthropy.

With their only child going to school in San Diego, Peter Martin and Sophia started spending a winter month in sunny Southern California to visit him. The senior Peter Wege called on MOF dealers in California—but he also found time to put a few dollars on horses at the Santa Anita racetrack.

A natural athlete, Peter Wege was a four-letter man at Brown Military Academy playing football, basketball, golf, and track. The muscular Wege was the Military Academy's designated weight man in track until the day he happened to watch California's best javelin thrower from Stanford working out. Peter went right to a sporting goods store and bought a javelin. Without any coaching, his first throws flew 150 feet. That's when the husky teenager knew he'd found his best sport.

Had Hitler not tried to turn the free world into his Fascist empire, Peter Melvin Wege might have become an Olympic athlete in the javelin throw. But history had a more important job ahead for Wege. Peter graduated from the Brown Military Academy in 1938 as a class officer and an admired athlete.

One of Peter's fellow cadets signed Wege's yearbook with prophetic advice: *If you keep up the pace you set here, I think you'll be a success in life.*

After graduating from Brown Military Academy in 1938, the year Kate Smith first sang Irving Berlin's *God Bless America,* Wege entered Lake Forest Academy in Lake Forest, Illinois, where he stayed until May 1941 and continued to excel at sports. He broke the high school's record for the javelin throw at over 180 feet setting a new record.

In September 1941, Peter Wege entered his freshman year at the University of Michigan. Because the Wolverine football coach had designs on the 6-foot tall, 185-pound freshman, Peter and his dad were given the royal campus tour by Michigan's legendary quarterback Tom Harmon. But flattered as he was by Harmon's attempt to recruit him, Peter Wege knew his gift was throwing the javelin.

Knowing the football team was hustling Wege, Michigan's track coach Ken Dougherty was mightily relieved when the brawny athlete showed up at Ferry Field to join the Wolverine track team.

That fall Peter, a new member of the Chi Psi Fraternity, set a new record for the longest javelin throw by a freshman in the University of Michigan's history, a feat not matched for 32 years. Wege's throw pierced the ground at 196' 6".

In fact, Wege's throw was so powerful that the javelin broke, with the spear and a piece of the splintered wood embedded in the ground—making it a legal toss. Peter retrieved the spear as a souvenir. But he was so excited about setting a record that he pitched the broken javelin too close to his bike and punctured the tire! The "conquering hero," as the Michigan fight song puts it, had to wheel his disabled bicycle back to the Chi Psi Lodge carrying the javelin trophy in his hand!

Sixty-six years later at a fund-raising event for Millennium Park, another Michigan athlete replaced that javelin. Greg Meyer, a Michigan track star and winner of the 1983 Boston Marathon, brought Peter Wege a javelin from the Michigan track coach painted maize and blue.

Greg Meyer said this about Peter Wege: *Peter represents everything Michigan strives to foster in its student athletes: intellectual curiosity, competitive drive, and a commitment to giving back. While there's no telling what marks Peter might have left at the University had the war not interrupted his stay, the marks he has left through his life serve as examples any athlete at Michigan would be proud to own.*

Peter's Michigan athletic career ended December 7, 1941, with the Japanese attack on Pearl Harbor. As with most Americans, Peter remembered exactly where he was when he heard the news. "I was driving my date back to Detroit that Sunday afternoon, and we had the radio on. I pulled over and heard the reporter say that President Roosevelt had declared war on Japan.

The next day, December 8, was my mother's birthday. I finished the semester and enlisted in the Army Air Corps. By April I was on a train to San Antonio where I lived in a tent for two weeks before the barracks were built."

Despite being their only child and with Peter Martin in his 70s, both Peter's parents supported their son's decision to volunteer. Although Peter Martin Wege was the son of German immigrants, he was a patriotic American. Indeed, after World War I, when his parents' native country Germany was defeated by the Allies, Peter Martin honored the United States by renaming one of Metal Office Furniture's first products, a bestselling MOF wastebasket he had designed. From 1918 on, MOF's steel wastebasket was sold as "The Victor."

And despite the fact their only child chose the dangerous duty of flying planes with the Army Air Corps, both parents supported their son's wish to fight for his country. In May 1943, First Lieutenant Peter M. Wege qualified to fly for the Army Air Corps.

Peter M. Wege graduates from San Diego's Brown Military Academy in 1938.

CHAPTER FOUR

EPIPHANY: THE WAR PILOT BECOMES AN ENVIRONMENTALIST

"CONSERVATION IS A STATE OF HARMONY BETWEEN MEN AND LAND."

ALDO LEOPOLD, *A SAND COUNTY ALMANAC*.
ECONOMICOLOGY: THE ELEVENTH COMMANDMENT,
PETER M. WEGE.

After graduating from flight school in 1943, Lt. Wege was delivering a trainer plane for fighter pilots to West Point when the view from the cockpit changed his life forever. Wege was approaching Pittsburgh to refuel when a black smog from the smokestacks of Pittsburgh's industrial plants engulfed his plane. In the middle of a sunny afternoon, the young pilot could not see the ground.

Wege later recounted, "I flew around the tallest building in Pittsburgh and asked the tower for a heading to the airport. Even after they gave me a heading, I still couldn't see it. They had to turn on the landing field lights before I could find the airport."

The shock of that pollution was an epiphany for Lt. Wege. Through his darkened cockpit, he understood what was happening to the world's clean air. That day in the pilot's seat of an AT-6, Wege's personal fight to save the environment began. And never ended. For the rest of his life, Peter Wege was to give passionately of his knowledge, energy, and resources to protect and preserve what he called "God's green Earth."

On July 14, 1943, while stationed in Atlanta, Georgia, Peter took a very special three-day pass to marry his hometown sweetheart, the pretty dark-haired Victoria Henry. He was 23, his bride two years younger. They had met on the beach in Grand Haven several years before. Vicki's parents, Dr. and Mrs. Frederick Henry, and Peter's parents were among the few guests attending their wedding in St. Anthony's Church.

But instead of a honeymoon, Lieutenant Peter Wege's orders took the newlyweds to Dallas, Texas, where he ferried planes around the country and world. From Dallas Lt. Wege was sent to Reno Army Base for training in the C-46. In late 1944, he was sent to North Africa.

As in "small world," en route to the North African Division Air Transport Command, Peter Wege ran into George Wells, a friend from Grand Rapids whose father Maurie Wells was the respected golf professional at Cascade Hills Country Club. George Wells was flying P-39 fighters to Alaska for Russian pilots to use against the Germans on the Russian front.

The two young pilot friends arranged to fly together from West Palm Beach to Accra, West Africa, but almost crashed on takeoff when their overloaded plane couldn't leave the ground. Wege and Wells got lucky again when their fuel had been miscalculated and they barely made it to land in Ascension Island in the South Atlantic Ocean.

Peter M. Wege enlisted in the Army Air Corps in early 1942 and served as a military pilot until 1946.

Fortunately in these two close calls, Peter Wege had special protection. Before he went overseas, his Saint Stephen's teachers Sister Leonard and Sister Vincent de Paul had given him a scapular medal crocheted in pink thread believed to hold a sliver of the cross. Not only did Lieutenant Wege carry the medal all through the war, he was never without it the rest of his life. However many new billfolds he bought, the scapular from his grade-school teachers was the first thing he put in it. The Sisters' scapular was in his wallet the day he died.

For the next two years, Lieutenant Wege flew transport planes in North Africa serving Tripoli, Oran, Khartoum, and Casablanca. Peter Wege's experience with the marvelous animals of North Africa over those two years deepened his love of Mother Nature and all her creations.

Peter Wege would become a lifelong supporter of the Natural Wildlife Federation. And fifty years later when Jane Goodall asked for his help to save Africa's endangered chimpanzees, Peter Wege's answer was easy. He'd seen the miracle of Africa's wildlife from a military jeep; he wanted to do whatever he could to preserve those magnificent animals for future generations.

And even as a young war pilot, Peter began doing "all the good" he could. The habit of giving he'd learned from his parents is documented in an early donation. Lt. Wege donated $100—a big check in 1944—to the Field Army American Cancer Society in North Africa. What Peter couldn't know was that both his parents would die of cancer within the next decade.

On September 2, 1945, Japan formally surrendered to the United States on board the battleship Missouri in Tokyo Bay with one of Peter Martin Wege's products playing a role. As the Japanese and American Naval officers were gathering on deck to witness Japanese General Yoshijiro Umezu signing the surrender, the Missouri crew saw they had a problem. The piles of documents wouldn't fit on the table they'd set up.

With true American resourcefulness, sailors ran down to the galley and grabbed one of the long mess tables made by Metal Office Furniture. They found a fancy cloth to cover the gray steel table and stood at attention while the two nations' naval officers ended World War II on an MOF table. Today that table made in Grand Rapids is a prized exhibit in the Historical Museum at the Naval Academy in Annapolis, Maryland.

The war was over and Lt. Peter Wege knew he was lucky to have survived it. But before going home, Peter found himself representing the United States in Istanbul for an international field event called the Balkan Relays. With no practice since his U of M days, Wege hadn't lost his edge, finishing second in the javelin throw to Steve Seymour, the world champion.

In November 1945, Lieutenant Wege got leave to go home for Thanksgiving to meet his baby daughter Mary Gretchen, born January 28, 1945. A thankful day for the Wege family when Peter held his ten-month-old Mary for the first time.

Two months later, on January 21, 1946, Lt. Wege was discharged and awarded the American Defense ribbon, the European Theatre Medal, and the WWII Victory medal. Peter was home from the war and this time he was there for the birth of his second daughter Susan Marie August 16, 1946.

Lt. Wege would forever be an ardent patriot and staunch supporter of the military. On Veterans Day November 11, 2000, when ground was broken for The National World War II Memorial in Washington, D.C., Peter and Steelcase representatives were invited as donors.

Flying with Peter in the Steelcase plane were six Steelcase retirees and WW II veterans along with Dick Becker, a retired Navy rear admiral and community relations executive for Steelcase. Peter and Dick had a special friendship through their Steelcase relationship. Indeed, Dick Becker would be asked to deliver the eulogy at Peter M. Wege's funeral in July 2014.

Watching the beginnings of the Word War II Memorial would prove to be an emotional day for the veterans from Grand Rapids. They were thinking about all their comrades who didn't come home.

In June, 1947, a year after Peter returned from the war, Peter Martin Wege, the father his son so admired, died of oral cancer at Blodgett Hospital. For the rest of his long life of giving, Peter Melvin Wege never stopped giving his father the credit. His standard response to thank yous for a donation was, "My dad's genius provided the resources so that I could do this."

Pilot Wege takes off for another mission during his four-year tour during World War II.

CHAPTER FIVE

POST-WAR FORTIES AND FIFTIES

"WE NEED TO LEARN FROM THOSE FUTURISTIC THINKERS WHO HAVE
TOLD US WE MUST BROADEN OUR VISION FROM THE NOW-ONLY FOCUS TO
A GENERATIONAL ATTENTION SPAN."

ECONOMICOLOGY: THE ELEVENTH COMMANDMENT,
PETER M. WEGE.

After the end of World War II, veterans returned home en masse, starting families, building houses, and going to college on the G.I. bill. New highways began the movement of families "out" to the suburbs, later described as "urban sprawl," an environmental challenge Peter would take on.

The 1944 Olympic Games Wege might have competed in with his javelin were cancelled because of the war. But in 1948 Peter's buddy Jim Delaney did win the silver medal in the shot, a feat Peter was always proud to tell people. After the war, Peter Wege rejoined Metal Office Furniture where he had worked summers. Only this time instead of the assembly line, he worked in product development and took his late father's seat on the board of directors.

The small plant his father had started 36 years earlier now had 535 employees. Peter Wege would sit on the board for 51 years, retiring in 1999 from Steelcase that was by then the largest office-furniture manufacturer in the world.

Peter and Vicki had been saving Peter Martin's name for their first son who arrived April 4, 1949. The new baby was christened for his late grandfather Peter Martin Wege II nicknamed "Peter Two."

After product development, Peter Wege moved to engineering and also created the company's first customer-service department. In 1952 he went on the road to call on MOF dealers through Pennsylvania and New York. Besides catalogues of his company's office furniture, in the back of his station wagon he carried one of MOF's C45 armchairs and one of their C48 swivel chairs.

In the early '50s, MOF began putting colors other than steel gray on office furniture and Peter's sales numbers went straight up. Instead of ordering the same boring gunmetal, customers clamored for the new shades of autumn haze, blond tan, and desert sage. Indeed by 1954, business was so good that the MOF's board of directors renamed the fast growing-company for its best known line of furniture, Steelcase.

In 1950 the United States Census was 150,520,198, up 19 million people in one decade. The population leap in this country and globally would become a major concern for Peter Wege. Already a committed environmentalist, Wege recognized the greatest risk to the planet would come from too many people drawing on the Earth's finite natural resources.

A sampling of news articles covering Peter M. Wege's gifts.

In the book he would later write, Wege cited the English economist Thomas Malthus on the danger of overpopulation. In *Economicology: The Eleventh Commandment*, Wege quotes Malthus: "Population, when unchecked increases in a geometric ratio. Subsistence increases only in an arithmetical ratio."

A good Catholic, Peter Wege nevertheless believed in and supported rational family planning in order to preserve Earth's limited natural resources. By the 21st Century, Wege's visionary outlook would be called "sustainability."

In 1959 at age 74, Lou Wege, Peter's "sainted mother," died from Alzheimer's and cancer. Over forty years later, her son would spearhead the founding of Gilda's Club, a cancer support club, to honor both his parents who'd died from cancer.

From the beginning of his career as a community leader in the 1950s, Peter Wege reflected the influence of his mother Sophia Wege. Her Catholic causes had become his. Father Flanagan's Boys Town was a home for needy boys in Missouri run by priests and that was enough for Peter Wege to support it. The Notre Dame Retreat House in Spring Lake and the Maryknoll Fathers on the East Coast were not local either, but they were Catholic.

Wege's two largest donations in 1951 were for Catholic missions. He gave his mother's parish, St. Stephen in East Grand Rapids, a generous $5,000 in 1951 dollars for the building fund. And he continued giving to Little Sisters of the Poor, a charity on the west side, because it "was my mother's favorite charity before she was married."

The same year of 1951 Wege was in church at St. Stephen when some fellow parishioners addressed the audience about the need to convert the Saint John's Orphan Asylum founded in 1889 from a home for orphans to a residence for neglected children. Peter's love for children led to an immediate $1,100 check. Later the same year Peter Wege again stepped up for children by donating $900 to Foster Parents for War Children so he could still help orphans.

Logos of several non-profits Peter and The Wege Foundation have donated to starting in the 1950s.

On October 6, 1951, Will K. Kellogg, creator of the first wheat cereals and a generous philanthropist, died in Battle Creek. Eighteen years later, in 1969, it would be a matching grant from the W.K. Kellogg Foundation Will K. had started that helped launch The Wege Foundation's first project: the Center for Environmental Study in Grand Rapids.

In 1952, Wege's fourth child Christopher Henry was born June 5. The same year a man destined to become one of Peter's visionary heroes Buckminster Fuller designed the geodesic dome. An inventor and philosopher, Fuller wrote about mankind's need to save Spaceship Earth before it was too late; his warnings would have a profound affect on Wege's own writings.

Peter Wege made two personal gifts in 1952 honoring the promise he made to himself flying over smoggy Pittsburgh during the war. One was for the National Wildlife Federation and the other for the Sierra Club of Grand Rapids, two environmental organizations he would increasingly support over the coming years. Indeed, the day was coming when Peter Wege would get selected to the National Wildlife Federation's President's Council.

While the environment surfaces early as Wege's driving enthusiasm, precursors to his passion for health care and preventive medicine also show up in his cancelled checks from the 1950s. Annual gifts to the Kent County TB Society, the Polio Foundation, the Muscular Dystrophy Association, and always, of course, the American Cancer Society.

The future direction of what would become The Wege Foundation's missions were already in play during the 1950s. Peter Wege would support causes that protected the environment, healed the sick, took care of children, and educated the public. Peter Wege's fourth cause, supporting arts and culture, began in the 1960s.

The depth of his passion for the arts would be manifested in 2002 when The Wege Foundation gave its single biggest gift of $20 million to the Grand Rapids Art Museum.

CHAPTER SIX

WEGE EMERGES AS A COMMUNITY LEADER

"THE PLANET IS A DIVINE GIFT. I SHALL NOT HESITATE TO DO WHATEVER I CAN TO KEEP IT WELL FOR THOSE WHO COME AFTER US."

PETER M. WEGE,
ECONOMICOLOGY: THE ELEVENTH COMMANDMENT.

As Peter was taking an active role in good causes during the 1950s, he and Vicki were also adding to their family. Chris Wege was born June 5, 1952, Diana three years later on October 13, 1955, and Johanna arrived February 9, 1958.

Devoted as Peter Wege was to his parents, it was no surprise that taking up the fight against cancer would be one his earliest commitments. In 1953 Wege took on his first of many leadership posts for the American Cancer Society. He co-chaired the annual ACS drive that raised $40,183—5% over the target. The ACS knew they had found a friend who could get the job done.

In 1955, Wege was elected president of the Kent County Unit of the American Cancer Society. This time Wege led the ACS to an all-time high in fundraising when he brought in $73,323. By 1959, the year his mother died of cancer, Wege would rise to the state's highest volunteer post for the ACS when he was elected president of the American Cancer Society for Michigan. Peter Wege was turning the loss of both his parents into an opportunity to save others.

Peter's experience with the ACS proved to him the importance of prevention and medical screening. He knew if his father had given up cigars and his mother's breast cancer had been found sooner, they would have lived longer. In one *Grand Rapids Press* news article, Wege praised the doctors in the Kent County Medical Society for their voluntary examinations at the ACS-funded clinic on Cherry Street.

But while the good Catholic hospital of Saint Mary's would always remain Wege's favorite, he did not hesitate to raise money for the other two acute-care hospitals in town: Blodgett and Butterworth. In 1958 Peter Wege and Frank Newman agreed to co-chair the corporate-giving committee in a three-hospital campaign called "The Good Samaritans."

The city-wide fundraiser enabled the city's three major hospitals to continue offering free health care to some 19,000 jobless families. Until then, the Community Chest had subsidized those medical costs. But in the 1950s, the combination of rising unemployment and higher medical costs had depleted those funds. The goal for the Good Samaritans campaign was $105,000 spread among three hospitals.

The Catholic Church elected a new Pope in 1958 with John XXIII and Saint Mary's Hospital got a new board leader when Peter Wege was elected chairman of the board of trustees. Saint Mary's knew they had a friend in their new chairman—but they had no idea what a good one Peter M. Wege would prove to be.

In 1961, ten years after Peter had first helped the former St. John's Orphanage become a home for abused and neglected children, the need to build new facilities arose. A new St. John's Home was needed for children suffering emotional and psychological damage by providing them with housing and intensive therapy in the context of love, hope, and respect for their dignity.

Again Peter was all in and in the fall of 1961, he was pictured in the Western Michigan Catholic magazine shoveling dirt with Albert F. Davis and Bishop Babcock in groundbreaking ceremonies for St. John's Home. Albert F. Davis, superintendent of the local GM plant, was a friend of Wege's and a fellow parishioner at St. Stephen's; together the two men had led the successful fund-raising drive to build a new St. John's Home.

This project on behalf of victimized children captured Wege's passion for young people and for education. Peter's son Chris Wege worked at St. John's over two summers. And even after St. John's Home became non-denominational instead of a Catholic home, The Wege Foundation continued to support it.

St. John's work of providing homes for needy youngsters where they could heal their hurts, keep them safe, and broaden their minds matched Peter's belief in holistic health, later embodied in the Wege Institute for Mind, Body, and Spirit.

Building a new St. John's did not distract Wege from the cause he had championed since his flight over Pittsburgh. Saving the planet was still his number-one mission. In 1962, he bought one of the first copies of a book that launched environmentalism into the mainstream making it a media topic for the first time. Rachel Carson's unexpected bestseller Silent Spring put her name on the front pages and made her an instant heroine to Peter Wege.

The biologist and naturalist had no idea her personal research into the loss of birds from DDT would have the national repercussions it did. Carson, now considered the founder of this country's environmental movement, woke Americans up to the fact that pesticides were killing off our wildlife and threatening human health. The huge success of Silent Spring unleashed the full fury of the powerful chemical industry that spared no money in castigating Carson as inept, immoral, and even crazy.

Two years after Silent Spring was published, Carson died of breast cancer at age 57. Following Rachel Carson's years of meticulous research into pesticides and the chemical destruction of nature, for the first time in history, the U.S. government began passing environmental laws.

In his 1998 book Economicology: The Eleventh Commandment, Wege would describe Rachel Carson as "a courageous advocate" who had spoken out "honestly on an environmental disgrace our national leaders had ignored." Three years after Rachel Carson's death, Peter Wege set up The Wege Foundation dedicated to preserving and protecting the environment.

In 2008, Wege invited the actress Kaiulani Lee to perform as Rachel Carson for the 12th annual Wege Lecture at Aquinas College. In the one-person play, A Sense of Wonder, the talented Lee "became" Rachel Carson—the marine biologist, poet, and lover of nature.

Aquinas College president Paul Nelson, Peter M. Wege next to his longtime friend President Gerald R. Ford, Sister Aquinas Weber, and Sister Marie Celeste Miller at the 2000 Emeritus dinner honoring President Ford.

Through the 1960s Peter Wege grew more active in the community. In 1969, he was named one of the first lay people invited to join Aquinas College's Board of Trustees. Wege would go on to serve the Aquinas Board for 13 years, completing his last three-year term in 2001. With the end of his official service in May of 2001, Aquinas Board unanimously elected Peter Trustee Emeritus for Life.

A former Boy Scout himself, in 1966 Peter Wege was elected vice-president of the Grand Valley Council, Boy Scouts of America. That same year the city of East Grand Rapids where Wege lived asked him to become a Citizen Leader. Over the years, whenever there was a need in East Grand Rapids, the elected officials would find their way to the Wege home, first on Lake Drive, and after 1968 to the house Peter built on Reeds Lake. East Grand Rapids' Citizen Leader didn't hesitate to support the city he and his children had grown up in.

In the mid-1960s, East Grand Rapids Mayor Donald O'Keefe named Wege to an eight-person advisory committee to study "the physical needs of the community and to recommend a program to meet the needs—including a new city hall." Peter served on the committee that ended up restoring the aging city hall.

Fast forward to August 11, 2006, and Peter Wege cuts the red ribbon to open a new city hall and library on the shores of Reeds Lake. Forty years after Mayor O'Keefe first got him involved, EGR's city officials would once again thank Wege both for his generosity and for his environmental vision that made sure the new city complex was built green.

Wege, however, wasn't done. He went on to give East Grand Rapids a green roof and solar panels for the library, new office space by recycling the unused water reservoir, and an environmentally protective walking trail around Reeds Lake.

The green roof and deck outside the East Grand Rapids Library overlooking Reeds Lake. On August 21, 2017, it was the gathering place for people to watch the solar eclipse. The smaller photo is the exit from the library to the green roof.

Then there was more. When the city fixed up John Collins Park on Reeds Lake, Peter donated a $160,000 water separator to filter out pollutants from storm water before it ran into the lake. While park visitors can't see this major infrastructure, it is critically important to the ecology of Reeds Lake as it cleans up polluted storm runoff before it can enter the lake.

The seventh and last Wege Jonathan Michael was born November 19, 1963. That same year his father set up the design, research, and development department for Steelcase, the company founded 51 years earlier by Jonathan's grandfather Peter Martin Wege as Metal Office Furniture. Peter Wege was also serving as the Corporate Secretary for Steelcase's Board of Directors.

And as the first Peter Martin Wege had established the values that would direct his company's generous treatment of employees, so would his son create Steelcase's environmental culture. The secretary of Steelcase's Board for over half a century, Peter Melvin Wege helped make Steelcase a national trail blazer in environmentally-friendly manufacturing.

It was Peter Wege's passionate advocacy for sustainability that spearheaded Steelcase's conversion to biodegradable paints, less packaging, cleaner air in the plant, and recycling, recycling, recycling.

CHAPTER SEVEN

PMW'S LARGEST GIFT BEFORE THE FOUNDATION

"Extinct is forever."

Christian Science Monitor on endangered species.
Economicology: The Eleventh Commandment,
Peter M. Wege.

On May 19, 1966, Peter Wege spoke at a dedication marking his largest bequest before starting The Wege Foundation. With Vietnam War protests waging at colleges across the country, Bishop Babcock and Aquinas College president Arthur F. Bukowski presided over joyful ceremonies on the small Catholic college's campus.

They assembled to dedicate Aquinas's first student center, a $750,000 building Peter Wege helped fund as a peaceful gathering place for Aquinas students. The Wege Center included an auditorium, a ballroom, a snack bar, bookstore, recreation center, and scattered lounges for study and socializing.

Already in 1966 Peter's environmentalism had made a convert out of Aquinas College President Monsignor Bukowski. Years later the green-wired Wege would still chuckle about the good priest "walking through the Administration Building at the end of the day turning off any lights left on." Peter knew the Monsignor's first thought was saving on electric bills. But he also knew Bukowski understood the environmental need to use less fossil fuel at every opportunity.

All the lights were blazing in the new student center on February 19, 1966, when 300 people hid behind the stage curtain. While Peter Wege thought he'd come to Aquinas for another meeting, his family and friends knew otherwise. Fortunately, Wege's healthy heart held up as the curtain was pulled and his favorite people in the world burst into, "Happy Birthday to you." Peter Wege was turning 46.

While Aquinas College was Wege's focus during the late '50s and early '60s, his active mind and heart were also engaged in other arenas. In addition to his determination to make Aquinas "the best small liberal arts college in the Midwest," the Corporate Secretary of Steelcase still made time to continue his work with the Boy Scouts, United Fund, the American Cancer Society, Saint Mary's Hospital, and to take a Trustee's seat on the Michigan Colleges Foundation. As if that wasn't enough, he also headed a campaign to raise funds for the St. Lazarus Retreat House in Spring Lake.

In 1965, to prepare for establishing his foundation, Peter M. Wege completed the legal proceedings regarding his inheritance that ultimately divided his personal fortune. Next, Wege felt free to put his remaining financial resources to work for the good causes he believed in. On July 13, 1967, the legal work was finished, and The Wege Foundation became a reality.

The tax benefits of the new family foundation enabled Wege to maximize his giving in his determination to make the world a better place. With this new charitable structure in place, Wege could put his assets, his intelligence, his energy, and his heart to work for the causes that touched his soul.

One hit song in 1967 could have been the theme song for launching The Wege Foundation: "All You Need is Love." Acting on his love for the planet, Peter Wege started The Wege Foundation that summer. As history would have it, the same year Peter M. Wege's heart opened his financial resources for others, the first human heart was successfully transplanted.

In what would become his signature statement, he described his philosophy: "Do all the good you can, in all the ways you can, to all the people you can, just as long as you can." The Wege Foundation was Peter's chance to do all the good he could in all the ways he could for all the people he could. As he recalled 30 years later, "I felt the need to set aside financial assets for the future needs of the community in which we live."

Undergirding that wish to help others was Peter Melvin Wege's determination to honor his parents and the legacy of humanity his father had instilled in the company he'd founded: Metal Office Furniture, now Steelcase. Scribbling and revising his dreams for the foundation on a legal pad in 1967, Peter Wege said it best himself.

"In the annals of history, no one has found a way to perpetuate a name better than creating a foundation. My father and mother are worthy of this honor. It also honors the descendants of that marriage. Peter Martin Wege was a man who understood the working man. He felt that if a man and wife worked hard for their survival, they should have a decent home, enough to sustain them with the necessities of life, and a chance for their children and grandchildren to have that also. That is why my father's family came to this country from Germany in the 1860s.

"Peter Martin Wege believed that a man should be able to go as far as his physical and mental capacities could take him. He also believed in a government, such as our own, that would provide for those who were destitute and otherwise unable to care for themselves.

"In the days of the Depression of 1929 and the resulting years of economic hardship, the company he founded would take care of as many workers as it could without the dissolution of the company. In other words, he believed in the responsibility companies had to provide for their workers until there was no hope. Then the government should provide sustenance until the family could recover. In order to perpetuate this philosophy, I think it's fitting The Wege Foundation should in perpetuity honor his name."

On August 3, 1967, in attorney Peter Van Domelen's office, Peter Wege chaired a meeting of The Wege Foundation to elect the first officers. Van Domelen had done the legal work setting up The Wege Foundation and between the two men they filled all the required offices. Wege was president, treasurer, trustee, and member; Van Domelen was secretary, trustee, and member. As secretary, Van Domelen kept the minutes of that founding meeting, recording that Mr. Wege wrote out a check for $1,000 to set up the Foundation's bank account.

The minutes outlined the "purpose of this Charitable trust" as receiving funds "exclusively for religious, charitable, scientific, testing for public safety, literary, and educational purposes." The future missions of The Wege Foundation were inherent in these goals.

Wege later clarified what he meant. "Research and testing for public safety in connection with the general problems of water pollution and air pollution for the welfare of the public in general."

Wege Foundation History 1967-2015

Peter Melvin Wege 1920-2014

One of Metal Office Furniture's first delivery trucks after the company's founding in 1912. In 1954, MOF would be renamed Steelcase for the product it was known for, seen on the truck here.

With major help from the W.K. Kellogg Foundation, Peter M. Wege started the Center for Environmental Study in 1968 supported by these community leaders. From the left beside Wege is David D. Hunting, one of the three founders of Metal Office Furniture along with Walter Idema and Peter Martin Wege. Next, Duane Kress, Phillip Nunn, Edward Stockton, and Neil Vierson III.

The Wege Foundation's first project was creating the Center for Environmental Study designed to clean up the polluted Grand River. Peter Wege's early commitment to protecting the wealth of Michigan's fresh water was a foreshadow of good works to come. Over thirty years later, in 2004, he would launch a national and international campaign to preserve and protect the waters of the five Great Lakes.

On March 19, 1968, The Wege Foundation held its first annual meeting, again at Peter Van Domelen's law office. Peter Wege added 28 shares of Steelcase common stock and $5,000 cash to the Foundation's bank account. The minutes from that day record the Foundation's three earliest grants—none surprising. Aquinas College received $2,861, Foster Parents $720, and the American Cancer Society $300.

The first Wege child to join the Foundation board was Peter's oldest daughter Mary Goodwillie who became a member and trustee April 24, 1968.

Peter's dream of a community environmental center to fight pollution was getting closer. But he knew what he envisioned wasn't going to be cheap, so he provided more of his personal assets. By March 4, 1969, The Wege Foundation recorded a total of 4,800 shares of Steelcase given by Peter Wege.

The Foundation was up and running, the funds were in place, and now the son of a bright and risk-taking father was ready to make his move.

CHAPTER EIGHT

PETER WEGE'S EARLY ENVIRONMENTAL BIBLE INSPIRES THE CES

"THE WAR TO KEEP MAN FROM SPOILING HIS ENVIRONMENT WILL NEVER END. BUT WE MUST REACH A POINT WHERE WE PUT PREVENTIVE ACTION INTO PLACE BEFORE THE DAMAGE IS SEVERE."

HEW SECRETARY JOHN GARDNER'S 1967, *STRATEGY FOR A LIVABLE ENVIRONMENT.*

In what would become the hallmark of The Wege Foundation over the years, Peter Wege's first undertaking was way ahead of its time—an environmental center. In those late 1960s, the news coverage was about Vietnam war protests, not the global threat to the future of the planet. Indeed, environmentalists were often dismissed as "tree huggers."

But fortunately some of this country's foresightful scientists *had* been paying attention. From 1965-67, a task force of scientific experts did an in-depth investigation on the health of the planet. President Johnson's Secretary of Health, Education and Welfare John Gardner chaired the task force. In 1967, two years before Wege launched the Center for Environmental Study, Secretary Gardner had published his final report. The title summarized the seriousness of the task force's findings: *A Strategy for a Livable Environment.*

Their conclusions were unambiguous. If Americans did not stop abusing the environment and destroying their country's natural resources, one day the planet would not be livable. John Gardner's report called on the federal government to work on a long-term strategy for saving the environment.

Tragically, government as usual meant the special-interest groups used their political clout to discourage Congress from acting on Gardner's report. The environmental laws needed to protect the Earth for future generations would have cost these private corporations money and inconvenience. Consequently, their paid lobbyists leaned on elected officials to tuck the report away in some remote file.

And the nation's elected leaders did just that. They ignored the task force's two years of study and did nothing. But in Grand Rapids, Michigan, one angry—yet caring man—did pay attention. Indeed, for the rest of his life Peter Wege referred to John Gardner's "Strategy" as "my environmental Bible." In 2007, Peter would still be giving away copies of John Gardner's book calling the author, "My environmental hero."

For the rest of his life, Peter talked about the thrill of actually meeting John Gardner in the 1960s. Peter never forgot their conversation. According to Peter, Gardner ended it by saying: "Move, Wege, move!" And so Wege did!

On August 8, 1969, with a $145,000 three-year matching grant from the W.K. Kellogg Foundation in Battle Creek, Peter Wege's longtime dream became reality. Partnering with the people from Kellogg, The Wege Foundation established the Center for Environmental Study (CES).

Peter Wege was deeply grateful to the people at W.K. Kellogg for their generosity in helping this important Center come to life. And typical of his modesty, Wege gave full credit to the Kellogg Foundation for the CES. He was also quick to say about their matching grant, "We made it last four years because we spent carefully."

Only three weeks before the CES was dedicated, two American Astronauts walked on the moon on July 20, 1969. Neil Armstrong, one of Gordy Varneau's friends, called his moon walk "one giant leap for mankind." Wege celebrated with the rest of the world… but it wasn't outer space he was worried about. It was Mother Earth.

The CES was Wege's first project to protect that Earth. The Wege Foundation's single biggest gift in 1969 was $3,000 to the Center for Environmental Study. The approach he used in starting the CES defined his style of doing charitable business for ever after: collaboration. Peter Wege went looking for kindred spirits who shared his environmental concerns.

He talked to friends, civic leaders, business people, educators, scientists, and anyone else willing to get involved. In the end, the two family foundations—Kellogg and Wege—were joined by thirty influential people and an advisory board of eight college presidents, including Aquinas president Dr. Norbert J. Hruby.

The people who said "yes" to Peter formed the CES's original Board of Trustees: John Adams, James H. Beaton, M.D., Harold E. Bowman, M.D., Wallace M. Chamberlain, Peter Cook, Winfred Ettesvold, Weldon D. Frankforter, Richard Gillett, J. Bernard Haviland, Leonard Hoffius, Duane Kress, Everett L. Ladd, Richard Lynch, William K. McInerney, Frank Neuman, Boris Palmer, John Pedden, M.D., Robert C. Pew, Winston B. Prothro, M.D., Joseph Renihan, Leonard Rosenzweig, M.D., James Sanderson, David Warm, Joseph M. Walsh, Peter M. Wege, and Theodore C. Williams with active participation by David D. Hunting and Dr. Henry Vaughn.

The members of this "brain bank," as Peter called it, committed to supporting the CES's mission of preserving, protecting, and improving the environment through public information. The CES's first location was Peter Wege's private office in what was then the Old Kent Bank Building.

On November 1, 1969, the CES moved into its own space on the fifth floor of the Exhibitor's Building. That year Sesame Street came on TV and in the mystic way life can come full circle, Peter Wege would one day meet the show's star, Kermit the Frog. They would come together some 25 years later in Southern California when Peter was honored for an environmental collaboration with the University of California. Peter Wege and Kermit would become immediate friends because, of course, they were both green.

The minutes of the first CES board meeting on November 17, 1969, reflect President Wege's priorities based on John Gardner's *A Strategy for a Livable Environment*. The minutes list the CES's top goals: "1. Air Pollution, 2. Water, 3. Solid and liquid wastes."

One of the CES's most effective educational outreaches was Biffo, the Environmental Clown who toured area schools using humor to teach children about the environment. From 1970 to 1973, Biffo gave his environmental fun show to 23,008 children in 71 schools.

At the same time, CES president Peter Wege and staff member Edward Stockton, environmental-quality project director, also hit the talk circuit on behalf of the CES. Between them, they spoke to meetings of Camp Fire Girls, Girl Scouts, Wyoming Lion's Club, and the YMCA, among other audiences.

Peter's talks zeroed in on what he saw as the main threat to the environment: an increasing number of humans drawing on the Earth's finite natural resources. Wege would go on to support family-planning programs because he saw the environmental necessity of parents being able to control the number of children they want. Wege never stopped talking to people about the environmental threat of over-population. A master at using humor to make his point, Wege's maxim was, "Educate, don't propagate."

Peter Wege was clearly ahead of his time in creating the Center for Environmental Study. Six months after the CES opened, America launched an historic environmental crusade. April 22, 1970, millions of men, women, and children across the country turned out for the first Earth Day. Wearing Earth Day T-shirts and waving green flags, these good citizens paraded across the land to raise awareness about the dangers to the world's ecology.

New York City closed Fifth Avenue for the Earth Day marchers. But what pleased Peter Wege most was the turnout in the nation's capital with ten thousand people at the Washington Monument forcing Congress to recess. Peter hadn't forgotten how the federal government had buried HEW Secretary John Gardner's environmental report three years before. Now Earth Day's ten thousand marchers in Washington would get the politicians' attention.

CHAPTER NINE

THE CES MAKES AN IMPACT

"Civilization itself is simply the advancement of human resources living in balance with nature's resources."

Peter M. Wege,
Economicology: The Eleventh Commandment.

At the September 1970 CES board meeting, Peter Wege read a letter from his friend and future President of the United States Congressman Gerald R. Ford endorsing the CES's pilot study of the Grand River to research water-quality management. And in the years ahead, Congressman Ford's younger brother Dick and his wife Ellen were to become two of Peter Wege's closest friends.

An editorial in The *Greater Grand Rapids News* dated September 30, 1970, described Peter Wege's role in the CES as "the founding father, the prime mover, and, let's face it, the guy who to date has footed most of the bills."

The editorial described Peter as "trying by private education to get government and average citizens to clean everything up so…man can have a better life." The writer noted that as a top Steelcase executive, Peter Wege had already put his company out in front as a pioneer in green manufacturing.

Economicology, the word Peter Wege created in the 1990s combining the words "ecology" and "economy," was already being tested at Steelcase in 1970, thanks to Wege's influence. Peter Wege used his word 'economicology' to explain that practicing good stewardship of the ecology also promotes the economy. As the President and CEO of the National Wildlife Federation Larry J. Schweiger later defined it, "In coining the term 'economicology,' Peter sought to succinctly express the concept that a healthy environment depends on a healthy ecology."

Steelcase demonstrated the merit of economicology when the office-furniture manufacturer bought an expensive bailing machine. Instead of polluting the air by burning tons of waste paper and cartons, the company founded by Peter Martin Wege invested in a machine to compress packaging cardboard and paper for recycling.

Steelcase proved the truth of Wege's theory of economicology in the real world when the bailing machine kept waste paper from landfills and also reduced expenses. Once it was paid for, the bailing machine saved Steelcase $20,000 a year.

The former Metal Office Furniture did even better in economicological terms when the company stopped putting used solvents into the sewers where it could enter the ground water. Doing the right thing for the ecology by reprocessing those solvents rather than dumping them saved Steelcase $60,000 a year and put the cleaned-up chemicals back to work in the plant instead of into the watershed.

It was no coincidence that in 1970 as Steelcase kicked into green manufacturing, the company posted its best sales ever of over $111 million. Peter Wege's faith in economicology was affirmed once more.

If Steelcase's environmental stewardship led the way, other good corporate citizens soon followed. The *Grand Rapids Press* did a story in October of 1971 on CES's honoring two local manufacturers for voluntarily spending money to reduce air pollution. Ralph Baldwin, of Oliver Machinery, and George Fischer, CEO of Grand Rapids Gypsum, were celebrated for investing in costly pollution-control equipment.

The news article quoted the CES's praise for what George Fischer's action had accomplished: "A white skyline has been traded for a clean air skyline at Grand Rapids Gypsum…white dust no longer settles on shrubbery and adjacent property."

In handing out the CES awards, Peter Wege presciently warned about the "serious health effects" of air pollution. In what would become a growing national health concern, Wege noted that dirty air was increasing the number of Americans diagnosed with asthma and bronchial diseases.

One of CES's causes aimed at burning yard leaves—which everyone did at the time—by educating the public on how those fires pollute the air everybody breathes. The message got through and, before long, burning leaves was prohibited and instead people bagged them for composting.

Along with curtailing air pollution, the CES moved forward on cleaning up the Grand River. In May 1971, the six mayors who formed the Association of Grand Rapids Area Governments asked Peter Wege and civic leader Jack Barnes to chair two Grand River clean-up drives. On two Saturdays in September of 1971, an army of local volunteers turned out for the clean-up.

By the end of the century, the United States Green Building Council would be a major player in both the environmental and the building communities. But thirty years earlier, CES had already discovered an expert in green design. On October 8, 1972, The *Grand Rapids Press* reported on a lecture by Dr. Ian McHarg titled, "Design With Nature" showing the interconnectedness of art, architecture, ecology, and all living things.

The CES also recruited young people to help tell their environmental story. In a newspaper picture from the early 1970s, nine girls from the Teen Board at Steketee's Department Store are holding copies of the CES's report on "Solid Waste Control" as they deliver them to area schools and businesses.

Another of the CES's notable successes was a 1973 noise-pollution study for Grand Rapids' City Manager resulting in the city's first noise ordinance. Working with the West Michigan Environmental Action Council, the CES helped the City Commission set legal noise limits for cars, trucks, factories, motorcycles, and musical instruments in public places.

In 1974, the CES did a computer-based simulation of the Grand River Basin's total environment, including both physical and human factors, for the Michigan Water Resources Commission. With the W.K. Kellogg Foundation grant having run its course, CES president Wege took on the $8,500 cost of this study, the biggest gift of The Wege Foundation.

The CES board, taking its lead from President Wege, continued to broaden its collaborative base. By 1974, the CES board included members representing the KISD, Chamber of Commerce, Public Museum, Junior League, Urban League, Grand Rapids Junior College, the Kent County Health Department, local physicians, engineers, and industrialists.

As one of the newspaper editorials prophetically said, "We will surely hear more of Peter Wege and his Center for Environmental Study in the future."

CHAPTER TEN

AN EARLY CHAMPION FOR WOMEN

"THE GREATEST GOOD IS WISDOM."

ST. AUGUSTINE. *ECONOMICOLOGY: THE ELEVENTH COMMANDMENT,* PETER M. WEGE.

If leading the Center for Environmental Study was Peter Wege's top priority during the 1970s, it was not his only interest. In addition to his seat on the boards of Aquinas College, Saint Mary's Hospital, and the Grand Rapids Art Museum, Wege took on one more board position as a father.

Peter Wege agreed to sit on the board of Marywood Academy, a Catholic school taught by the Dominicans, for one reason. "My four girls all went to kindergarten there," he explained.

The seventies also saw the start of the movement referred to as "women's lib." But The Wege Foundation had already given $500 to help start the Women's Resource Center helping women finish their educations, find employment, or get training for a better job.

In 1973 Peter Wege again reached out to women in need by helping buy a home on Lyon Street for women recovering from substance abuse. The Wege Foundation's pledge of $1,500 helped start Our Hope that continues giving hope to women struggling with alcoholism and addiction.

Peter Wege stepped forward for other "feminine" causes by donating to The League of Women Voters and the Women's Committee of the Grand Rapids Symphony. Particularly progressive was Wege's support for family planning by giving to Planned Parenthood. Indeed, his environmental Bible, John Gardner's 1967 report, *A Strategy For A Livable Environment,* says this: "Population problems compound all the other environmental threats to man."

But his most personal, long-term commitment to a woman's organization started in 1972, and not only honored women, but also his Catholic faith, his passion for the environment, and his advocacy for education. It began when the Sisters of Mercy, owners of Saint Mary's Hospital, invited seven Franciscan sisters to move from Cicero, Illinois, to Grand Rapids and start a center for handicapped children in a rural setting.

Led by Mother Superior Rita, the Franciscans moved into Mercy Hall where the Sisters of Mercy also lived. Several Franciscans, including nurse Sister Patricia, began working at the hospital. As Providence would have it, Sister Patricia's specialty in treating diabetic patients would bring Peter Wege into the Franciscans' lives.

It began when one of Sister Patricia's patients was a little dark-haired boy named Jonathan Wege being treated for juvenile diabetes.

As Peter Wege visited his son in the hospital, the appreciative father asked Sister Patricia why the Franciscans had come to Grand Rapids. When he heard what they were called to do,

The yurt at the Franciscans' Life Process Center.

Peter Wege saw a match made in heaven. Children with special needs getting educated in an outdoor setting. It wasn't long before Sister Patricia and Wege were driving east of town looking at farms for sale.

They found the perfect spot in Lowell. Using his personal money rather than The Wege Foundation's funds, in 1972 Peter bought the Franciscans a 212-acre farm in Lowell. Wege hired his friend architect Hans Weimer to design a building for the Franciscans to live in—including a small chapel—and classrooms for preschoolers.

As Weimer broke ground for the Franciscans in 1973, Peter Wege's friend and Congressman Gerald R. Ford unexpectedly became Vice-President of the United States. The dream-becoming-reality for the Franciscans in their peaceful bucolic setting stood in sharp contrast to the country's distress over Watergate that didn't end until President Nixon resigned in 1974. And then Peter's friend, the new President Gerald R. Ford, from Grand Rapids could tell the world, "Our national nightmare is over."

For the Franciscans, the original building of what would become several more at 11761 Downes Road in Lowell welcomed the first class of five preschoolers in 1975. As more students enrolled, so did the Franciscan Sisters expand their program to include music education and music therapy. In 1979, they began a musical outreach teaching classes in an Ada studio called Franciscan Rhythms. And since Sister Mary Margaret was a talented baker, in 1980 the Franciscans added a bakery and coffee shop to the studio.

Sister Ann, one of the early Franciscans in Lowell, would later reflect on the magnificent outreach that began at the hospital bed of a diabetic child and became the Franciscans Life Process Center. "It was a spiritual way in which one thing led to another." The warm and supportive relationship between the Franciscans

Franciscan Sister Damien Marie in a field of wild flowers at the Life Process Center.

in their long brown robes and Peter Wege grew stronger over the years. Their shared Catholic faith was the starter. But what touched Peter most about these women whose lives were so different from his was their deep love of the Earth. In 2003 Peter Wege brought his family and friends together to celebrate his 83rd birthday party at the Life Process Center.

Peter later gave the Franciscans two yurts to help house their spiritual retreat guests. The Franciscans' circular, tent-like yurts with heated sleeping quarters, hardwood floors, a bathroom, and views of a woods rich with wildlife have become popular places for church retreats.

Franciscan Sister Jo Ann with Peter M. Wege

CHAPTER ELEVEN

THE WEGE FOUNDATION EMBRACES CONSERVATION IN COSTA RICA

"TO STRIVE FOR ENVIRONMENTAL QUALITY COULD BE CONSIDERED THE ELEVENTH COMMANDMENT." RENE DUBOS.

ECONOMICOLOGY: THE ELEVENTH COMMANDMENT,
PETER M. WEGE.

As The Wege Foundation spread its wings to include more good works, Peter did not forget his earliest charities. In 1973, The Wege Foundation's second largest grant of $8,000 went to Aquinas College.

A $500 gift to the Michigan Colleges Foundation in 1969 reflected Peter's ongoing support for all causes educational. The MCF is made up of small private colleges, including, of course, Aquinas. The Wege Foundation's grant to MCF went to scholarships for students who otherwise couldn't afford those schools.

On May 13, 1970, with The Wege Foundation offices housed on the 5th Floor of the Exhibitors Building, Peter invited his second oldest child and oldest son Peter Martin Wege II to join The Wege Foundation Board of Trustees. The records of that annual meeting pointed to Peter M. Wege's growing interest in the social and educational needs of the inner city. The Foundation gave $500 to the Grand Rapids Urban League and the same amount to the Vocational Skills Center.

And the Foundation's $1,000 to help the Grand Valley Council of Boy Scouts build a new camp indicated Wege hadn't forgotten his Boy Scouts either. With his sons in the Boy Scouts, Peter was always a major donor. But three decades later, Peter would again prove his even-handedness. In 2003, when the Michigan Trails Girl Scouts needed to expand their Camp Ann Behrens in Greenville, Peter made sure the girls got his help as the boys had when he pledged $250,000 for the Girl Scouts' camp.

In 1970, with his new Foundation in place, Peter Wege pledged $1,000 to the University of Mchigan, his first major gift to the school that began a long-term friendship between Michigan and The Wege Foundation centered on the environment.

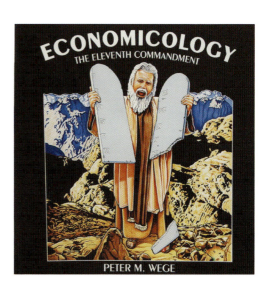

The cover of Peter M. Wege's first book on economicology by the late environmental artist Mark Heckman.

In the spring of 1971 when Peter attended his son Peter's graduation from Williams College, the commencement speaker, microbiologist Rene DuBos, made a powerful impact. Thirty years later, Peter Wege had not forgotten DuBos's call for Williams' new graduates to nurture the living Earth because it shapes and determines man's fate.

Indeed, in 1998 Peter would borrow a phrase from Rene DuBos for his own book *Economicology*. Rene DuBos had written: "To strive for environmental quality could be considered the eleventh commandment." On the cover of *Economicology* above Mark Heckman's rendition of Moses holding a tablet with I-XI laws is the sub-title: *The Eleventh Comandment*.

Not surprisingly in the early 1970s, Peter Wege got involved with a new non-profit called the West Michigan Environmental Action Council (WMEAC). Started in 1968 by a group of citizens who shared Wege's environmental concerns, WMEAC's mission dovetailed with his. Like The Wege Foundation, from the beginning, WMEAC's members helped educate the public to "make a difference in the environment" for future generations.

In 1977 Peter began supporting a small environmental school in Cedar Springs called Jordan College.

Founded in 1967 as a two-year Bible college, by the time The Wege Foundation got involved, it had ended its religious affiliation and was renamed Jordan College. What attracted Wege was the school's environmental curriculum offering associate degrees in the science of alternative-energy.

From the beginning, Peter Wege had written and talked about the world's diminishing supply of fossil fuel and the imperative need to develop newer, cleaner energy. Wege saw Jordan College's emphasis on solar energy as the way of the future. The Jordan students built solar heating units that warmed two of their buildings and went on the road teaching people how to build their own solar heating units.

As a Jordan College board member, Peter Wege enthusiastically supported the school buses that brought children from kindergarten through high school to the campus teaching them how solar energy works. Jordan College was ahead of its time in recognizing the need to teach young people about solar energy.

The Wege Foundation continued to support Jordan College until the late 1980s when the school closed. By then, however, the many students and homeowners educated by Jordan College had already stepped into the future by learning how to create cleaner and safer renewable power through solar energy.

Peter Wege's support had helped make that vital education happen. Wege's belief in solar power only grew stronger after the Jordan College years. Over time, Peter Wege would contribute solar panels to several major buildings, including the Jarecki Center at Aquinas, East Grand Rapids City Complex, and a new environmental building at the University of California, Santa Barbara.

Wege was ahead of his time not only in his visionary support for solar energy, but also for recognizing the dangers of using nuclear power for energy. In 1979 Peter Wege wrote a letter to Consumer's Power in Jackson, Michigan, warning the company about the risks. Wege noted that "when man designs a technology to produce power, it is a man-made technology and subject to error."

He pointed out that the nuclear-power leak at Three Mile Island demonstrated this very fallibility. Wege told Consumers that the next nuclear "incident" might not be lucky enough to "avert disaster" and could leave behind "a wasteland."

His warning about "a catastrophic backlash of radiation" proved to be tragically prophetic." Seven years later, on April 26, 1986, a fire broke out in the Soviet Union's Chernobyl nuclear power plant contaminating much of Europe with radioactive fallout. Peter Wege's recognition of environmental dangers others couldn't—or wouldn't—see made him something of a Cassandra. Fated to tell the truth but not to be believed.

As the list of grant requests to The Wege Foundation increased every year over the 1980s, so did the amount and breadth of Peter Wege's giving. Yet he never took his eye off The Wege Foundation's first cause: the Center for Environmental Study.

By 1984 the CES was losing momentum and Wege knew it needed retooling. He called on Grand Rapids Community College's President Dick Calkins to discuss some collaboration, and Calkins willingly opened the college's doors to the CES. More important, he came up with a dynamic new director named Kay Dodge to reenergize the 15-year-old CES.

Kay Dodge was an experienced ecology teacher with a PhD from Michigan State University and a passion for the environment. She was a natural to take over the CES. Gratified by the CES's new dynamics, Peter and The Wege Foundation continued to send quarterly checks of $15,000-$20,000. In 1990, Wege noted on his pledge list that $100,000 a year to the CES should continue "until further notice."

Under CES's mission of International Projects, in 1986, Kay Dodge organized a trip to Costa Rica that had an historic effect on Peter Wege and The Wege Foundation. Along with bird watching and the stupendous views of Costa Rica's rain forests, the group discovered that little Costa Rica was becoming the most progressive country in the world on land conservation.

Wege was an instant supporter—morally, scientifically, and financially—of the two government officials driving rain-forest conservation. The combined bold leadership of Costa Rica's president Oscar Arias and his First Minister of Natural Resources Alvaro Umana to protect their nation's tropical environment matched Wege's own passion for planet Earth.

The Wege Foundation began its first out-of-country funding to support the daring vision of the Costa Rican heads of state. "The world's rain forests provide 26 percent of the oxygen we breathe," Wege was quick to say about his commitment to the Central American country's conservation movement.

While The Wege Foundation's Costa Rican involvement started with Arias and Umana, it wasn't long before an American biology professor from the University of Pennsylvania took over as point man. Dr. Dan Janzen and his wife Dr. Winnie Hallwachs also shared the conservation dreams for Costa Rica where they'd moved for Janzen's scientific research.

Dan and Winnie Janzen were destined to become good friends of Peter Wege, and together they would help triple the conserved land map of Costa Rica. Peter's and The Wege Foundation's contribution to that effort over the coming years would add up to well over $5 million.

Another major benefit of the 1986 CES trip turned out to be the young college student named Terri McCarthy who was Kay Dodge's assistant on the tour. Three years later, in 1989, Peter would hire Terri to help the Franciscan Sisters raise $1.8 million so they could expand their preschool and integrate it with senior citizens.

Terri left the Franciscans to teach biology at Greenville High School until Peter offered her a full-time job in 1998 as the program officer at The Wege Foundation, doubling the staff headed by Ellen Satterlee who had been the director since 1988. Starting with her first day at work in February 1998, Terri knew her job was not going to be dull. Terri McCarthy came to work for Peter Wege the day Steelcase went public.

As it happened that momentous day in 1998, both Peter and Ellen were out of town. That left Terri alone in the office taking calls from business reporters around the country wanting a comment from Steelcase's biggest stockholder. In a baptism by fire, Terri McCarthy was now part of the team in the generous, compassionate, and wonderful world of Wege.

Listing Steelcase as a publicly traded company on the New York Stock Exchange would lead to more of The Wege Foundation's generous and compassionate deeds. When Steelcase went public in 1998 Wege and a trust held for his benefit sold $214 million of stock, most of it earmarked for the Foundation.

Thus, overnight, The Wege Foundation's assets would almost triple. For Peter Wege and The Wege Foundation, that meant only one thing. Now he could give away three times as much money to the causes of his heart.

Formerly Saint Mary's hospitals, now Mercy Health Wege Institute for Mind, Body, & Spirit, Mercy Health Lacks Cancer Center, and Mercy Health Hauenstein Neuroscience Center.

Photo: Lacks Cancer Center

CHAPTER TWELVE

HEALTH CARE, THE UNDERSERVED, AND ELLEN

"All men are by nature equal, all, of the same earth by the same Creator and… as dear to God is the poor peasant as the mighty prince."
PLATO.

ECONOMICOLOGY: The Eleventh Commandment,
Peter M. Wege.

Saint Mary's Hospital would always be Peter's favorite as a board member and donor. But it wasn't the only health-care program in town blessed by his generosity. In 1985, Wege gave $50,000 to build a new blood center on Fuller Street, the high-tech, sophisticated Michigan Community Blood Center. Then in 1989 he pledged $1 million of the total $2.2 milion cost to buy a magnetic resonance imaging unit—the MRI.

This state-of-the-art diagnostic machine uses a magnetic field with radio waves rather than x-rays enabling doctors to see inside the body. Supporting Wege's advocacy for collaboration, this mobile MRI was shared by five Grand Rapids hospials: Blodgett, where Wege's father had been treated, Saint Mary's, of course, Butterworth, Osteopathic, and Ferguson.

But it was not just the needs of the physically ill that touched Peter Wege's heart. He might have been the only child in a privileged family, but Peter Wege was keenly sensitive to the hurts of his city's most vulnerable people. As the 1980s moved away from institutionalizing mental-health patients and began mainstreaming them into their own communities, Peter Wege was right there to help.

In 1985 he donated $200,000 for a new facility called Sojourners Transitional Living Center to care for head-injury patients. The Wege Foundation also supported a new program called Transitions to help people suffering from mental and emotional disabilities. Because of generous supporters like Wege, Transitions could give disabled people, who once would have been locked up, the chance to become productive citizens by helping them find homes, transportation, and jobs.

In a December 2004 interview with a West Catholic High school student named Tristan Johnson, Wege gave an answer that helps illuminate his outreach to the people most in need of help. For the article Tristan was writing about Wege for the school paper *Westword*, Johnson put this question to the then 84-year old philanthropist: "You have played year-round Santa for most of your adult life. What would you like today's young people to understand about the importance of giving?"

Without hesitation, Peter replied: "Your gift may well be a time in a person's life…which will be a turning point—a point in their lives that will give them confidence to survive and carry on in a positive way and become a positive force in helping the community prosper."

Peter Melvin Wege 1920-2014

Ellen Satterlee, Executive Assistant to The Wege Foundation 1988-1998. Executive Director 1998-2010. President 2010-2015.

Wege's belief in "turning points" and second chances is also behind his giving the YWCA $25,000 to start a program for victims of childhood sexual abuse. If society too often overlooked these unfortunate men and women, Peter Wege never did. Instead he supported those organizations that could offer the most help in bringing them from despair to hope.

The people and the needs of the city, too, were always high on Peter Wege's caring screen. In 1988, he donated $75,000 to build a new swimming pool for the YMCA. In August 1989, he pledged $30,000 to support the inner-city schools through the Grand Rapids Public Education Fund. Another $5,000 went to Grand Rapids Urban League and $3,000 to Grand Rapids Jaycees Family Park.

Peter Wege's largest and most influential gifts to the inner city were yet to come and would be focused on two neighborhoods. And his interest in both of them was as personal as it was powerful.

In 1986 Peter M. Wege retired from Steelcase giving him more time to serve The Wege Foundation. But after trying to handle his new full-time job giving money to good causes, he realized he needed help. In May of 1988, Peter asked Steelcase to quietly send over the three best people on the company's list of temporary executive assistants.

The first one to be interviewed was a bright, blue-eyed young woman named Ellen Satterlee. Before giving Ellen the name and address of the person who was going to interview her, Steelcase's human-resources executive told Ellen she was being considered for a "highly confidential" job "outside Steelcase."

When Ellen found out who it was, she called her husband Gale who also worked for Steelcase and asked him to guess what Steelcase executive wanted to interview her. "Not Frank Merlotti," Gale said in shock, naming the president of Steelcase at the time. "Higher," Ellen said.

"You don't mean Bob Pew!" Gale said in disbelief as he named the president of the Steelcase board. When Ellen said he still wasn't there, Gale gasped. The only Steelcase executive outranking the CEO and board chair was the company's major stockholder: Peter Wege.

The morning of the interview, Ellen asked Gale to drive her as she had no idea how to find Reeds Lake Boulevard and didn't want to be late. Yet nervous as she understandably was, Ellen Satterlee had solid credentials of her own. She'd worked four years for the top executives at Zondervan Publishing and now had a promising career at Steelcase.

Ellen had also lost her adored father Gilbert Cotter the year before, and her three sons were growing up fast. She had made up her mind she would only do what was best for her and for her three teenaged boys. Waiting for Peter in the office wing of his Reeds Lake home, Ellen saw why he needed help.

All available surfaces in the two office rooms were covered with jumbled piles of papers, magazines, and letters. Organizing this chaos into a working office was right up her alley. Yet exciting as this opportunity might be, Ellen Satterlee had two requirements of her own: a starting salary she could live with and a schedule that got her home by 4:30 for her sons.

With his ability to size people up in a hurry, Wege saw this friendly, articulate, attractive woman as exactly the person he was looking for. Not even bothering with the other two interviews, Wege offered her the job on the spot. He agreed to her hours, but not her salary request. Earlier in her life, Ellen would have accepted Wege's offer at less than she knew she was worth. But she'd had a hard year, and she was stronger.

It was a defining moment in what would become a symbiotic relationship that helped both Peter Wege and Ellen Satterlee become more than they would have been without each other. Sweet, gentle, soft-spoken Ellen looked Peter Wege straight in the eye and said, "No thank you."

Accustomed to calling the shots, Peter Wege did not like being told what he should pay his new assistant. But he also knew a good thing when he saw it. Reluctantly, grumblingly he accepted her salary request. And from that first meeting on, Ellen Satterlee's ability to stand her ground in the kindest possible way proved to be one of the strengths that served The Wege Foundation best. She soon realized a big part of her job would be telling hopeful grantees their request for funding had been declined.

Until his death in July 2014, Ellen Satterlee was Peter Wege's right hand. And in his last few years of failing health and for the year after he died until she retired in October 2015, Ellen was Wege's public representative. While she never forgot he was her boss, neither did Peter ever underestimate her strength in being her own person. Their respect for each other created the synergy that led The Wege Foundation to becoming one of the most powerful forces for good in West Michigan.

As The Wege Foundation grew from $4.7 million when she started to $175 million within ten years, the funding applications rose proportionately. This escalation of grant requests gave Ellen Satterlee more chances than she ever wanted to exercise the talent Wege discovered the day he met her. Ellen Satterlee had the uncanny ability to tell grant seekers "no" so nicely that they almost felt like it was a "yes."

CHAPTER THIRTEEN

EVERYONE IN HEARTSIDE KNOWS WHO PETER IS

"Everyone in this two-block area knows who Peter Wege is."
Denny Sturtevant, CEO, Dwelling Place

In 1989, the free world celebrated as the Cold War officially ended November 10 when the Germans tore down the Berlin Wall. Peter Wege, the pilot who'd done his part to defeat tyranny in World War II, was jubilant over the liberation of Eastern Europe. But it didn't distract him from what needed to be done in his hometown.

By the end of the 1980s, Peter Wege saw with dismay the growing deterioration along South Division where his parents had lived and the original Metal Office Furniture plant was located. This Heartside neighborhood, an area south of Fulton settled by Dutch immigrants in the late 1840s, was near the train station. But after World War II when new superhighways replaced the need for train travel, Heartside's hotels and businesses fell on hard times.

In a serendipity that so often happened for Wege, his vision for the Heartside corner and another good cause came together with harmonic timing. Across the street from his parents' former apartment at 359 South Division on the corner of Wealthy, an expanding Catholic Central High School was crowding out administration offices.

When Dave Seamon, director of the Catholic Secondary Schools at the time, brought this to Peter's attention, Peter and Sophia Wege's only child had the answer. He would buy the building where his parents had lived across the street from the high school and make office space for the Catholic Secondary Schools.

The $1 million Wege gave to help the Catholic schools met three personal goals. First, Wege was supporting the Catholic education his mother Sophia Dubridge Wege believed in. Second, Catholic Central High School was where all his Dubridge cousins had gone to school. Third, he was rescuing his father's first home in Grand Rapids from crime and decay.

A newspaper photo of the refurbished building at 359 S. Division shows a handsome Victorian structure with snappy striped awnings over vintage oriel windows. When it was done, the first tenants were Ellen Satterlee and The Wege Foundation where The Foundation offices stayed for several months.

Around the time Wege was redoing his parents' apartment building, a young man named Denny Sturtevant entered Peter's life. It was the beginning of a special relationship between two good men who cared deeply about the inner-city's neediest residents.

In 1989 Dennis Sturtevant took over Dwelling Place, a non-profit organization formed by area churches in 1980. A group of downtown churches, Degage' Ministries, and Saint Mary's Hospital started the Dwelling Place when the upscale development of downtown triggered by the new Amway Grand Plaza hotel began. The organizers saw that the coming gentrification could leave many Heartside residents no longer able to afford their rent.

Peter Martin Wege's first home after moving to Grand Rapids in 1911 was a second-floor apartment in this building at 359 South Division at Wealthy. After Peter Martin's marriage to Sophia Dubridge, it was their home and where they brought their newborn son Peter M. Wege in 1920. In 1989 Peter's devotion to his parents led him to rehab this building for the Catholic Secondary Schools. A few years later as he looked at it from across the street where he was being honored by the Catholic Diocese for a generous gift, Peter thought about his parents and stood up abruptly to announce he was giving the church another major donation.

A news article from the early 1990s recognizing the successful renewal of several Heartside buildings thanks to Peter M. Wege and The Wege Foundation working with Denny Sturtevant and Dwelling Place.

As developers bought and raised prices on more downtown property, the people living south of Fulton Street were increasingly at risk for homelessness. Dwelling Place's mission was to preserve affordable housing for Heartside's low-income residents. And when the non-profit faced a financial crisis, it was Peter's father's company Steelcase and the Grand Rapids Community Foundation that bailed out Dwelling Place giving it time to stabilize operations.

Not long after that crucial support from Steelcase and the GRCF, Denny Sturtevant and Peter Wege teamed up to create affordable housing by purchasing and restoring properties in Heartside. Their first property was the Lenox Building next to the one Peter had already bought for the Catholic Secondary Schools. Now the Catholic schools' offices needed more parking spots so Peter bought them this second building for parking places behind the Lenox Building.

After buying the Lenox Building from Wepman's Pawn Shop, Wege called Ken Hoexum, First of America Bank president. Wouldn't it be a wonderful show of faith in renewing Heartside, Peter asked Ken, if his bank opened a branch in the Lenox Building? Recognizing Peter's efforts to support more affordable housing and bring businesses back to a safe Heartside, Hoexum agreed to do his part. Before long an FOA branch office opened on the first floor of the Lenox Building.

Now that Peter had acquired and fixed up the first two buildings north of Wealthy for the Catholic Secondary Schools, the run-down buildings next door from 337-341 Division looked even more dilapidated by comparison. Peter's and Denny's next move was to buy another eyesore building in this same block intending to tear it down. But because the vacant building was in an historic district, the plan to raze it fell through.

Instead Peter agreed to donate the building to Dwelling Place and connect it to an adjacent one Dwelling Place already owned. With Peter's and The Wege Foundation's generous funding for renovations, these two buildings were turned into fourteen affordable one- and two-bedroom apartments. Rehabbing these buildings also opened up commercial space that ultimately became Dwelling Place's offices and the Heartside Grocery.

As have so many grateful recipients before and after, Dennis Sturtevant wanted to thank Wege by naming one of the buildings after him. And, as usual, Peter respectfully declined. Sturtevant remembered what Wege said in turning down this honor. "Peter told me, 'When I'm long gone, the legacy will be in this building that we've partnered on.'"

"Peter wants these buildings themselves, not his name on them, to serve as his commitment and support," Denny Sturtevant said. "But don't think those most affected by his generosity and vision don't know. In this two-block area," Denny Sturtevant said with emphasis, "*everyone* knows who Peter Wege is."

It was the kind of tribute that meant the most to Peter—and most honored his generous heart.

CHAPTER FOURTEEN

GIVING AWAY THE SAME BUILDING TWICE

"I BELIEVE THAT MAN WILL NOT MERELY ENDURE. HE WILL PREVAIL...BECAUSE HE HAS A SOUL, A SPIRIT CAPABLE OF COMPASSION AND SACRIFICE AND ENDURANCE."
WILLIAM FAULKNER, NOBEL PRIZE SPEECH 1949.

ECONOMICOLOGY: THE ELEVENTH COMMANDMENT,
PETER M. WEGE.

Because of Peter Wege's extraordinary generosity to Dwelling Place, Denny Sturtevant was understandably reluctant to ask for any more help. But he didn't have to. Peter would call Sturtevant periodically to ask if he needed anything. That's what happened in 1991 when Wege called and this time Denny said there was a need. God's Kitchen feeding the inner-city's poor and homeless had to be redone and it would cost $100,000.

"How much is The Steelcase Foundation giving you?" Peter asked. Denny told him Steelcase had already given so much financial support to keep the Dwelling Place open during their financial crisis that the Steelcase Board had declined the latest request for God's Kitchen.

Peter's response was to tell, not ask, Sturtevant, "Send it in again."

Embarrassed, Denny called the Steelcase Foundation explaining what had happened and that he wasn't trying to do an end run. The Foundation executive, a friend of Peter's, laughed and said she understood. And, of course, this time God's Kitchen got the grant they'd asked for from Steelcase.

Peter Wege's habit of calling Denny to see what he needed was also the way The Wege Foundation pledged $200,000 to help buy and restore the dilapidated Herkimer Hotel in the early 1990s. The run-down hotel was one block north of where Peter had started fixing up South Division.

But despite Peter's gift combined with other contributions, the $5 million Herkimer deal almost collapsed—wiping out the huge sums already invested in it. At the last minute, one of the sellers insisted on $22,000 in immediate cash to hold the option. Dwelling Place had neither the money nor enough time to raise it.

Denny knew only one person he could call on a moment's notice to save the Herkimer project. Peter Wege wrote the check that day. In 1995, the Herkimer's 14 newly remodeled apartments for low-income renters were dedicated at a summertime party.

In fact, it was this housewarming for the Herkimer that led to the best Wege-Sturtevant story. Peter knew Denny wanted to buy the Lenox building from the Catholic Secondary Schools so the Dwelling Place could renovate the upper floors for affordable housing, keep the bank, and upgrade the former Wepman Pawn Shop space for retail. Peter also knew the Catholic School officials had agreed Dwelling Place could buy the Lenox Building for whatever the appraised value turned out to be.

So over appetizers the night of the Herkimer dedication, Peter asked Sturtevant the status of the Lenox Building. Denny told him the sale fell through when the CSS decided the appraisal of $100,000 was too low a price and wouldn't sell it. If Denny Sturtevant thought this party conversation was the end of the matter, he was wrong.

Within days Denny found himself at a meeting in the Lenox Building under discussion. Around the table were the head of the Catholic Secondary Schools, the bankers, Peter Wege, and Ellen Satterlee. Wege and Ellen Satterlee were the only ones who knew why they were there.

Without preamble, Wege asked CSS Superintendent Dave Seamon, "If I offer you $100,000 for this Lenox Building we're in, will you take it?"

The Catholic educator was caught off guard. But considering that Wege had bought and restored the building as a gift to the Catholic Secondary Schools in the first place, Seamon had really only one answer. Of course he'd take any offer Wege made.

While Denny Sturtevant had nothing to do with how the two Lenox transactions came about, it became one of Peter Wege's favorite stories about Dwelling Place's CEO. "This is the only man I know," he'd say pointing at Denny, "who could get me to buy the same building twice and give it away both times."

But true to form, buying the building back from CSS and giving it to Dwelling Place was not enough for Peter. He showed up one day in Denny's basement office in the Lenox Building and said it was too dark. "You need some greenery around here." Driving down South Division today, one might never realize that the first trees planted on that strip of Heartside in half a century grow there because Peter saw an absence of green.

Denny Sturtevant, CEO of Dwelling Place, and Peter M. Wege's friend and partner in rehabbing South Division buildings to provide affordable housing.

The snowball effect of what Peter and Denny started in the Heartside neighborhood in 1989 has led to more upgrades along both sides of the street. That's exactly what both men wanted to happen. As Peter put it, his longterm plan was to rehab the area "all the way to Wurzburgs."

A few years later, Denny Sturtevant got a surprise phone call from Peter asking for a favor. "I'm coming with my hat in my hand," Peter said. While Denny couldn't imagine what he could ever do for Peter, one thing he knew for sure. Whatever it was, Denny would do everything in his power to make it happen.

Peter's "favor" involved The Wege Foundation's support for building the Richard J. Lacks Cancer Center at St. Mary's. The Lacks project had hit a wall when St. Mary's wanted to tear down the original hospital in the McAuley Building to make room for the new cancer hospital. The Grand Rapids Historical Commission opposed tearing down the McAuley. Peter knew Denny Sturtevant had faced this challenge before.

Denny's "favor" was using his Dwelling Place experience to call members of the Historical Commission he had worked with before on similar conflicts. Gradually, with some give and take on both sides, the Historical Commission agreed to the demolition. The McAuley Building came down so the Richard J. Lacks Cancer Center could go up. Denny still carries the thrill of having done a favor for the man who had given so much to Dwelling Place.

Liz's House, a shelter for women and children, the Heartside Grocery, the Herkimer, God's Kitchen, the Goodrich, the Lenox—blocks of Heartside all had reason to be named for Peter Wege. But over his half-century of giving, naming opportunities never mattered to Peter Wege.

He once tried to explain this to a *Press* reporter who wondered what motivated his endless generosity. "If we aren't here on Earth to solve problems," Wege answered, "what are we here for?" For Peter Wege, the city neighborhood known as Heartside is named exactly what it should be.

CHAPTER FIFTEEN

A HELPING MINISTRY AND A HELPING SCHOOL

"PETER WEGE IS ONE OF THE MOST WARM-HEARTED PEOPLE I HAVE EVER MET."
PASTOR BARBARA PEKICH.

Peter Wege's heart proved big enough to soon embrace another good cause in the Heartside neighborhood. Started in 1983 and operating out of a decrepit building at 54 South Division, the Heartside Ministry is a storefront chapel and a place where people come in from the street for spiritual comfort and human caring.

In the late 1980s George Heartwell, who later became mayor of Grand Rapids, was the pastor of Heartside Ministry. By that time, as Heartwell put it, "Peter Wege's philanthropy on behalf of Dwelling Place was legendary.

"So I thought," Heartwell later recalled about his approach to Wege in 1999, "Peter is a friend of mine. I've never asked him for money for Heartside before. Maybe now is the time."

Heartwell therefore prepared what he described as "a modest grant request for about $70,000 to provide mental-health services for people living in Dwelling Place facilities." Since the proposed counseling would be done at the Heartside Ministry, Heartwell invited Peter to a meeting in that building.

"From the time he and Ellen Satterlee came into our crowded, well-used quarters," Heartwell recalled, "the gears in Peter's mind were turning. Finally he couldn't hold back any longer. "This place looks terrible!'" Wege told Heartwell and Reverend Barb Pekich, Heartwell's co-pastor who later took over for Heartwell.

"If you want to dignify your people," Wege said of the poor and homeless and mentally ill who find daily sanctuary there, "then give them a place that says you dignify them."

Like Heartwell, Pastor Barbara Pekich has vivid memories of that meeting with Peter Wege and Ellen. "It was my first encounter with Mr. Wege's wonderful personality and his leadership in recognizing a bigger problem. He told us to dream a beautiful space for our people, and I've been in love with him ever since."

Looking back on that 1999 day, Mayor Heartwell said, "Peter began to spin a vision for a new space with natural daylight, warm, inviting colors, vastly improved service-delivery facilities, and, of course, a host of environmental improvements."

"But, Peter," Heartwell recalled finally breaking into Wege's excited commentary on gutting and redoing the building, "this all sounds fine. But we really need to talk about this $70,000 mental health grant."

Peter Wege didn't pause. "Ellen," he said to Ellen Satterlee, "write him a check. Now let's talk about fixing this place up." And he went right back to planning a total renovation of the space including converting an alley loading dock into a meeting room.

Heartside Ministry at 54 S. Division describes itself as "a place for people to escape the drama of being on the streets with nothing to do. It's a place for learning, receiving help, congregating, socializing" and worshipping "if you so choose."

"Before he left that day," Heartwell said, "Peter had not only given what I had asked for, but pledged another $40,000 for architectural changes to support the mental-health services that I hadn't even thought of."

What happened next was classic Peter Wege. He'd been as moved by the Ministry's mission caring for the city's neediest souls as he was distressed by the facility where they came for comfort. Right out of the chute, he pledged $250,000 for the renovation and hired a consultant to help raise another $1.875 million.

With Wege already on board, Peter Cook, Steelcase, Grand Rapids Community, and Frey Foundations soon followed. With none of the fanfare and press photos that often accompany philanthropy, Peter Wege made sure the full $1.9 million was raised in a campaign titled, "The Heart of the Matter."

Heartside Ministry continues to offer programs in its bigger, brighter, barrier-free, wired new space, where over 100 area residents come daily for activities, art, friendship, and ministry. They also have the opportunity to get computer training, exercise classes, and receive counseling for substance abuse and domestic violence.

But Peter Wege was also looking into the future for this spiritual and social center vital to the people of Heartside. Besides the expansion and upgrades, he saw to it that $1 million went into an endowment to make sure the Heartside Ministry had money for needs yet to come.

Pastor Barbara Pekich could have been speaking for all the street people who come to Heartside Ministry and are dignified by Peter Wege's vision for "beautiful space" there. "Peter Wege," she said, "is one of the most warm-hearted people I have ever met."

Lake Michigan Academy was founded in 1985 by Grand Rapids parents of children with learning disabilities who needed to be taught according to their individual "learning differences".

Peter Wege wasn't done in the Heartside district. In 2000, The Wege Foundation supported renovation of an abandoned building on Commerce built in the 1800s as the Heysteck Auditorium. Over the next century it had declined into a roller rink, auto-parts store, and finally a garage.

Wege saw this Heysteck project as a community win-win. A Heartside eyesore would become an asset and bring dream tenants into the neighborhood. The Heart of West Michigan United Way proved his point when they moved in to be closer to the clients they served.

At the dedication of the renovated building, Michael Brennan, United Way's director at the time, told Peter Wege, "You have always been fundamental to United Way…those who are homeless, victims of child abuse, substance abusers—your passion has always been to help the neediest."

On the front wall of the renovated Heysteck Building's entrance is a quote by Peter Wege: "The United Way", Peter's words read, "means collaboration of all agencies for the common welfare." Collaborating with other non-profits was always Peter's way of doing business.

In the spring of 2005, the City of Grand Rapids, with the former Heartside Ministry pastor George Heartwell now Mayor Heartwell, voted to spend $2 million renovating Heartside's streetscape. The city's decision to enhance Heartside's sidewalks carried on the renewal of the neighborhood Peter Wege had started in the 1980s.

On November 9, 1999, another of Peter's quiet kindnesses would change the lives of young people coping with a learning challenge. And, like so many of his gifts, it began with a friendship. Peter's friend Chuck Stoddard, founder of Grand Bank, invited Peter to a fundraiser called the Chuck Roast. Because Stoddard was known for his terrible puns—and Peter loved them all—the dinner proved to be standup comedy for the 300 laughing guests.

The dinner's mission, however, was serious—raising money for Lake Michigan Academy, the school Chuck and Jan Stoddard had helped start in 1985 for children with learning disabilities. The need for such a school was obvious by the late 1990s when LMA's two rented buildings at Aquinas College weren't big enough.

In 1999, as luck would have it, a like-new charter school came on the marketspace—exactly what Lake Michigan Academy needed. It was this charter school's $2 million asking price that led to the fundraising Chuck Roast. Calling Peter Wege "one of my heroes," Stoddard recalled his shock the night of the dinner when Wege said he would match whatever funds were raised. Thirty-two thousand immediately became $64,000.

But Peter wasn't done. The garrulous Chuck Stoddard was struck speechless when his friend Peter announced that The Wege Foundation was also donating $500,000 to the LMA's capital campaign. A helping hand for children dealing with a challenge. Education. A friend. Lake Michigan Academy had all the strings needed to tug at Peter's heart as well as meeting The Wege Foundation's mission.

Peter Melvin Wege 1920-2014

CHAPTER SIXTEEN

AQUINAS EXPANDS AND PUBLIC TRANSPORTATION INCREASES

"WE HAVE FORGOTTEN HOW TO BE GOOD GUESTS, HOW TO WALK LIGHTLY ON THE EARTH AS ITS OTHER CREATURES DO."
STOCKHOLM CONFERENCE, 'ONLY ONE EARTH.' 1972.
ECONOMICOLOGY: THE ELEVENTH COMMANDMENT,
PETER M. WEGE.

Even as Peter Wege began his outreach to the inner city in the late 1980s, his stewardship of Aquinas College never faltered. From 1955 to 1981, the gifts to Aquinas from The Wege Foundation and from Peter Wege's personal account totaled $446,000.

And then in 1989 Peter Wege moved into seven figures for Aquinas when he kicked off an $8 million fund drive with his lead gift of $1 million. The largest capital campaign in Aquinas history built a new library and updated science equipment.

But the most important piece of that fund drive added 17 acres and 11 buildings to the college when Aquinas's neighbor the Reformed Bible College needed to expand. The Bible College offered Aquinas an opportunity the school couldn't turn down.

As the Reformed Bible College moved to the East Beltline and renamed itself Kuyper College, Aquinas launched its $8 million "Aquinas Grows" drive to buy the Bible College's Robinson Road property. With this major expansion, the Dominican sisters had come a long way since 1922. That was the year Dominicans founded Aquinas as Sacred Heart on Fulton. In 1931, the Dominicans moved Sacred Heart downtown to 69 Ransom and renamed it Catholic Junior College.

Walking back and forth to Catholic Junior College from their Marywood home during the 1930s, the Sisters passed—and dreamed about—the Edward and Susan Blodgett Lowe estate on Fulton. Then, in the depression year of 1938, the 69 acres and 22-room Tudor mansion went up for sale at much less than it was worth. But the nuns still couldn't afford it.

In a remarkable tweak of history, the sisters called on a man they'd heard "was a good and generous benefactor" to consider helping them buy Holmdene, the name of the Lowe estate. Peter Martin Wege accepted their invitation to visit Marywood and discuss the possibility. Over tea, the senior Wege agreed that the Holmdene estate—the McCoy dairy farm when the Lowes bought it in 1905—was ideal for the Dominicans' college.

But before the 68-year-old Peter Martin Wege could act, the for-profit Grand Rapids University bought the Lowe estate for $85,000.

Certainly the good sisters weren't *happy* when GRU (where President Gerald R. Ford taught law and coached football) failed in 1945. But this time they moved fast. For less than $150,000 they bought Holmdene from Grand Rapids University and renamed it for Saint Thomas Aquinas.

Grand Rapids Mayor Rosalynn Bliss helps cut the ribbon on a new sidewalk along 28th Street that enables people in wheelchairs to get around their neighborhood no longer having to roll through dirt paths.

After Peter's and The Wege Foundation's spearheading the purchase of the Bible College's campus, Aquinas College President Norbert Hruby described his college's most generous friend: "Peter Wege is a guy who takes the world seriously. I think he's used his money to good effect without spending his time with the jet set…all he wants to do is bring peace to the world and improve the environment."

In 1993 Peter found a new way to "improve the environment" and help those in need by supporting a newly formed organization called Disability Advocates. As the name implies, this non-profit's purpose is giving people with disabilities access to the same opportunities able-bodied people have. The mission of this spin-off from Hope Network is to help disabled people "live full and exciting lives."

Disability Advocates prepares their clients for employment, makes sure their homes meet their needs, and helps them map out personal goals. Yet given all that, what if the disabled person can't reach the places necessary for meeting those goals? To lead "full and exciting lives" they need to get to jobs, school, social events, religious services.

Thus one of Disability Advocates' first projects was improving public transportation so that people with a disability who are unable to drive or can't afford lift-equipped vans can get where they need to go.

The low-key philanthropist Peter Wege always had a heart for people with tough challenges. And because Kate Pew Wolters, his good friend and fellow descendant of the Steelcase founders, was a passionate advocate for people with disabilities, Peter became one too. In 2000 the Rapid put its first millage request before voters called Faith in Motion. The YES vote was supported by a collaboration of leaders in the religious community, business executives, and supportive citizens calling themselves Friends of Transit.

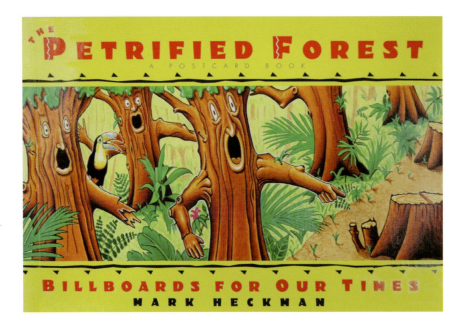

One of the billboards by the late environmental artist Mark Heckman sponsored by Peter and The Wege Foundation.

According to Dave Bulkowski, executive director of Disability Advocates, "Peter Wege's $40,000 contribution that year to the Friends of Transit campaign was absolutely indispensable. His leadership and generosity enabled us to get the public's attention with billboards and flyers and mailings."

And the campaign's colorful billboards were created by Peter's friend and environmental artist, the late Mark Heckman. The first Rapid millage passed by a wide margin. But more needed to be done for expanded bus service with longer hours. Peter Wege didn't hesitate to lead again.

In 2001 he pledged $40,000 a year for three years to Faith In Motion; in 2003 he again helped fund the successful campaign that added routes and hours to bus service. Peter continued his substantial support for better public transportation every year until his death in 2014. The Wege Foundation has carried on that support for Disability Advocates and public transportation with the total donations into 2016 of $695,000.

And this long-term support triggered another bonus. Because of The Wege Foundation's high credibility, The Mott Foundation came on board in 2013 pledging $120,000 over three years to support public transportation in Kent County.

By 2016, the public could see the tangible results of Peter's and The Wege Foundation's generous support for public transportation. That's when Michigan's first high-capacity transit, the Silver Line, went into service carrying more passengers more frequently to more distant destinations.

Peter Wege saw improved public transportation as a demonstration of economicology by getting workers to their jobs and reducing the carbon pollution individual cars emit. Whether they know it or not, every bus rider going to work is practicing economicology.

While Disability Advocates and its community partners still need to extend transit service beyond Grand Rapids, they know the community owes an unpayable debt to Peter for his perseverance and commitment to a better future for all.

"When you see a bus out at night," Dave Bulkowski says with a grateful grin, "you can thank Peter Wege."

CHAPTER SEVENTEEN

WEALTHY BUSINESS DISTRICT'S RENAISSANCE

"BY ALLOWING NONREPLACEABLE NATURAL GOODS TO GET SQUANDERED AND BY ALLOWING THE POPULATION TO GROW UNCHECKED, WE PUNISH THE CHILDREN TO BE BORN IN THE NEXT CENTURY."

ECONOMICOLOGY: THE ELEVENTH COMMANDMENT,
PETER M. WEGE.

If restoring the Heartside neighorbood began with Wege's personal history there, so did his gift of a former theater to another inner-city neighborhood on Wealthy and Fuller. Wealthy Theatre had once been that business district's main attraction—even claiming its own streetcar stop.

Opened as the Pastime Vaudette in 1911, the ornate theater featured live entertainment. But even then, vaudeville was fading and during World War I Pastime closed its doors. The theater's large spaces were used to store equipment for the new Michigan Aircraft Company.

In 1920, the Pastime reopened as Wealthy Theatre. The new owners of the freshly painted baroque movie house were Oscar and Lillian Varneau, parents of Peter Wege's best friend Gordy, and like second parents to Wege. When they got old enough, Peter and Gordy earned a healthy twenty-five cents an hour ushering movie goers to their seats.

By the late 1950s, Wealthy Theatre's audiences began to decline. The flight to the suburbs, the growth of television, and new big movie screens outside the city slowly put the neighborhood theater out of business. In 1973, Wealthy Theatre closed its doors.

The boarded-up building finally became a public hazard. As one city commissioner told the *Grand Rapids Press*, it was where "druglords and gangs ruled." In 1989, the city of Grand Rapids decided to demolish Wealthy Theatre.

That announcement mobilized the area's residents and business owners into action to stop its destruction by forming a non-profit called the South East Economic Development. They knew razing the theater would further damage the appeal of a once vibrant business district. SEED's first move was successful as they convinced the city to declare Wealthy Theatre a designated historic landmark and then sell it to the non-profit for a dollar.

The second move, however, was daunting. It would take several million of those one-dollar bills to repair the damage done over the 14 years of vacancy and vandalism. SEED had one shining hope. They knew Peter Wege to be an environmentalist who believed in restoring, not destroying. They also knew about his generosity bringing new vitality to the Heartside neighborhood.

Both good reasons to approach Wege. But for the best reason, the SEED leaders had no idea about. Peter Wege had strong personal feelings about Wealthy Theatre because for him it meant Gordy Varneau and the Varneau family. And to a man who cherishes his friends, the chance to honor the Varneaus was all Peter had to hear.

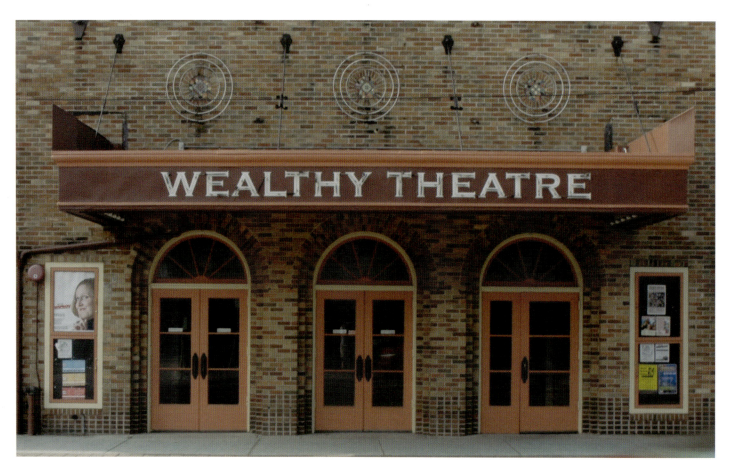

Restored and reopened in 1997, Wealthy Theatre triggered the rejuvenation of the Wealthy Business District. Peter M. Wege had special feelings for the Theatre because it had once been owned by his best friend Gordy Varneau's parents whose name in mosaic tiles is still in the lobby.

Peter Wege led the charge to raise the $2.2 million for restoration. In 1997, Wealthy Theatre reopened as a performing arts center with the lobby's original mosaic floor. At the entrance, clear white tiles against a red background still clearly read, VARNEAU.

For Wege, the highlight of the occasion was having his friend Gordy fly in from Las Vegas to join the dedication. "Gordy's been my best friend since we were in kindergarten together at St. Stephen's School," Wege told the media. And Gordy, usually the jokester, was visibly moved when he saw what Wege had done for his parents' theater.

But Wege wasn't done with the stretch of Wealthy Street where he and Gordy had spent their Saturday afternoons. A dilapidated party store up the street from Wealthy Theatre was a known place to deal drugs. Peter decided the only way to clean up that corner was to buy the store himself. In the fall of 2000, The Wege Foundation bought the 3,000 square-foot junk building and the run-down, two-story house behind it.

Wege's goal was to restore the southwest corner of Wealthy and Fuller to the people who lived in the neighborhood and owned businesses there. Not wanting to own the corner property himself, Peter knew just the guy to give it to. Denny Sturtevant knew how to manage inner-city real estate, and the non-profit Dwelling Place he headed took ownership of the former drug corner.

As Sturtevant told a reporter, "Peter has got such a good attitude about gifts like this. I've seen philanthropic gifts before, and these have always had the giver's mission involved—that things had to be done a certain way. But Peter comes in and does things like this without having a clue how it's all going to end up, but knowing something needs to be done. Peter leaves that to the community and the neighborhood to figure out how it can be done best."

While Wege turned the deeds over to the Dwelling Place, he also asked the neighbors to do the planning for the property themselves. The people who lived and worked in the Wealthy Street neighborhood accepted Wege's offer—and challenge. They called themselves SHOWtime! 2001—Something's Happening On Wealthy. And it all started with Wealthy Theatre.

Dottie Clune, a Dyer-Ives Foundation consultant overseeing SHOWtime!, described the significance of Peter Wege's actions. "The convenience store project was an impetus to bring a lot of people together because Peter Wege had asked for community input on the eventual use of that building. And he wanted to make sure that we didn't look at just that building, but put it in the context of the whole street."

As many as 50 people from the Wealthy Theatre area came to the SHOWtime!'s community meetings because they knew Peter Wege was behind the project. As Sturtevant put it, "When people hear that Peter Wege is involved, all of a sudden their expectations get raised."

Thanks to The Wege Foundation, in place of ugly graffiti scrawled on boarded windows on the Wealthy-Fuller corner, the neighbors got handsome green-and-white striped awnings. In place of a drug-dealing store, the neighbors got an education center run by Grand Rapids Community College.

Wege gave GRCC a $35,000 grant and $9,000 to cover the Dwelling Place's year lease of the building then-GRCC president Juan Olivarez said his college's mission was offering "exposure and outreach" to both "kids and adults." The goal of the GRCC's Learning Corner was to promote literacy in life skills, academics, and technology.

Denny Sturtevant called the community college's move into the former convenience store "one more link in forging the chain of healthy neighborhood revitalization." He said of Peter Wege's role, "Peter stepped up to the plate, and he wants others to participate."

Pedestrian traffic soon increased as people felt safe once more shopping and dining on Wealthy Street. In 2002, Huntington Bank moved into the refurbished space next door to the Learning Center.

Barb McClurg and Melissa LaGrand opened Wealthy Bakery that soon became a hot spot for lunches and homemade breads.

JR's Deli, Lorina's, Divine Divas Salon, Screenbeater Silkscreen, Rhodes Rib Crib, Verhey Carpets, and Sandmann's brought more people into the Wealthy Street business district giving new life and spirit to what Wealthy Theatre had started.

In the summer of 2004, with the Community Media Center now in charge of the theater's operations, Wealthy Theatre Wireless opened to offer free Internet access to people without computers or without Internet. The Community Media Center also donated computers to five households living in the Wealthy Theatre Wireless area.

The Wealthy Theatre neighbors knew exactly who had jumpstarted the rebirth of their street. In 2002, the Wealthy Street Business Alliance honored Peter by awarding The Wege Foundation the title of providing the "Best Program In Response To An Issue or Need."

Two years before this award, Peter Wege had given the commencement speech to the first Aquinas College students to graduate in the new millennium. He focused on the beliefs and attitudes that made Wealthy Street happen telling the college seniors to get beyond how "it's always been done…believe in your own power to make the 21st Century better than the last."

Peter concluded with a classic pun. "We don't need more icons. We need more 'I cans!'"

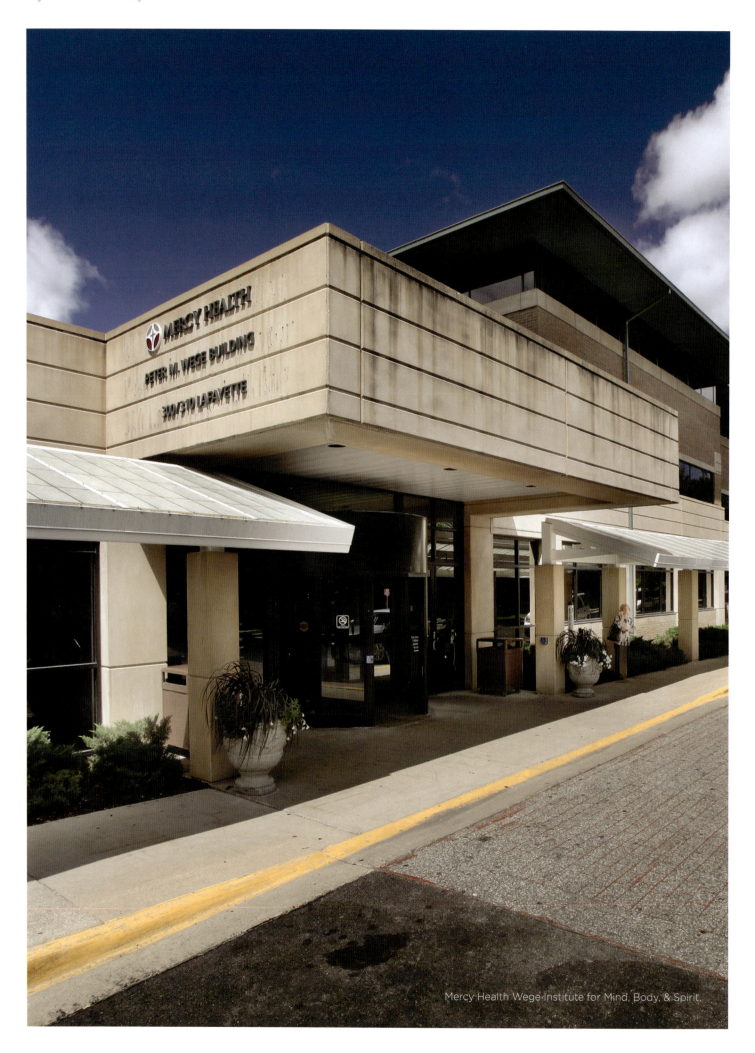

Mercy Health Wege Institute for Mind, Body, & Spirit.

CHAPTER EIGHTEEN

THE HOSPITAL OF HIS HEART

"WHAT THE LATE 20TH CENTURY IS REDISCOVERING ABOUT THE
INTEGRATION OF EACH INDIVIDUAL AS A UNITY OF MIND, BODY, AND SPIRIT,
TEILHARD DE CARDIN WROTE ABOUT IN *THE PHENOMENON OF MAN* IN 1955."

*ECONOMICOLOGY: THE ELEVENTH COMMANDMENT,
PETER M. WEGE.*

One of Peter's "I cans" took place in the late 1990s at Saint Mary's Hospital. As the only child of a devout Catholic mother, he'd been deeply moved when his mother told him how she'd prayed to the Virgin Mary during the difficult delivery when he was born there. Over his lifelong commitment to Saint Mary's, Peter Wege would contribute over $30 million to the hospital his mother loved.

One of Peter Wege's own "I cans" would change the practice of health care at the hospital of his heart. In 1998 Wege asked Saint Mary's to move beyond traditional medicine. Wege challenged the hospital staff to treat the whole person instead of limiting medical care to the disease itself.

Having studied the efficacy of certain Asian medical therapies, Peter Wege urged Saint Mary's to add complementary healing to its science-based medicine and to promote holistic health. A sound mind in a sound body with a strong spiritual component. Startling at first, Saint Mary's President and CEO at the time David Ameen realized Wege was moving the hospital toward a wellness approach already being quietly practiced by mainstream Americans.

The result of Wege's vision was a new $16 million building for Saint Mary's named for what it did: The Institute for Mind, Body, and Spirit. And in one of the few times Peter Wege acceded to having the Wege name attached to one of his gifts, it is called the Peter M. Wege Institute. "I agreed only because it's my father's and my son's name too," Peter made clear lest one think he named the building for himself!

Philip McCorkle, who followed Ameen as Saint Mary's president and CEO, summarized Wege's role in the hospital's major leap forward into complementary medicine. "Peter has clearly directed us onto paths that have changed the way we do business. His insistence on attention to complementary health practices and the integration of mind, body, and spirit in our medicine led to the development of the Wege Institute which now provides the model of care in our hospital. And not only our main hospital, but also our Center for Diabetes and Endocrinology, and our new Mercy Health Lacks Cancer Center."

John Gardner's 1969 HEW Report that Peter Wege called his "environmental Bible" also influenced Wege's forward-thinking support for preventive medicine. HEW Secretary John Gardner's 1969 Report stated: "…environmental protection must be based on a new view of the relationship of man, health, and the environment—namely, that human illness can be a symptom of environmental disease, and that environmental health efforts must treat or prevent the disease itself, not the symptom."

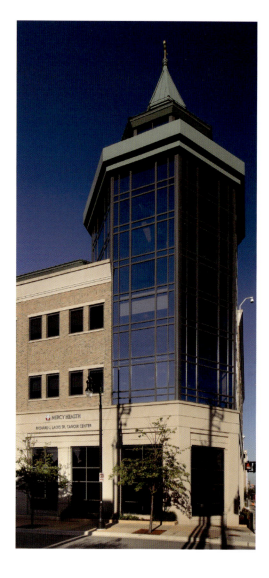

Mercy Health
Richard J. Lacks Cancer Center

Preventive medicine and holistic healing became hallmarks of Wege's health-care advocacy. But his progressive thinking was always in addition to traditional medicine, which he soon proved with a significant gift to Saint Mary's for a new cancer center that he supported for three classic Peter reasons.

First, he loved Saint Mary's where he and five of his children were born. Second, he had long been a warrior against the disease that took both his parents' lives. But finally, and maybe most important, this gift was about a lifelong friendship. Mary Jane Morrissey Lacks and Peter had been classmates at St. Stephen's. They were born the same year in 1920 and they died within a month of each other in 2014.

So when the Richard J. Lacks family wanted to honor him by building a cancer hospital in his name, Peter M. Wege signed on with a $16.5 million gift. But beyond his donation, Peter Wege's vision influenced how the Lacks Cancer Center was built and how it would be run.

Wege made sure Saint Mary's applied to the U.S. Green Building Council's official award system. Called Leadership in Energy and Environmental Design (LEED), the certification process required the Lacks Cancer Center to follow strict guidelines covering construction from site preparation to water-saving plumbing, and from energy-efficient heating to recyclable materials.

Peter Wege also encouraged the staff in the five-story Lacks Cancer Center to treat each patient as a whole person physically, mentally, emotionally, and spiritually.

The resulting Richard J. Lacks Cancer Center is not only friendlier for the planet and healthier for the patients, but the 180,000-square-foot hospital also made LEED history. In 2004, the Lacks Cancer Center became the second hospital in the country to earn LEED certification from the United States Green Building Council.

Formerly Saint Mary's hospitals, now Mercy Health Wege Institute for Mind, Body, & Spirit, Mercy Health Lacks Cancer Center, and Mercy Health Hauenstein Neuroscience Center.

Mercy Health Hauenstein Neuroscience Center.

The $42 million Richard J. Lacks Cancer Center—now Mercy Health Lacks Cancer Center—went up on the land Denny Sturtevant's 'favor' for Peter made available. Denny was able to broker a deal with the Grand Rapids Historic Preservation Commission to allow the demolition of the original hospital.

On the heels of the Lacks Center, Wege stepped up with a third major Saint Mary's gift to help build a neuroscience center and, once again, because of a close friendship. Ralph Hauenstein, his fellow Catholic and World War II veteran, wanted to open a hospital devoted to neurological diseases like Parkinson's and Alzheimer's.

The five-story, $60 million Hauenstein Neuroscience Center incorporated Wege's model of high-tech medicine in the context of holistic health to treat neurological diseases and brain injuries. And as with the Lacks Center, if Wege is involved, the Neuroscience Center's applying for LEED certification was a given.

Peter Wege's generosity and vision would continue to influence every future Saint Mary's building project as shown in their Byron Center hospital. At one point hospital president Philip McCorkle actually offered Peter what many philanthropists would jump at asking if they could name the "the whole hospital" after him. Wege wasn't even tempted. Putting the three generations of Peter M. Weges on one wing of Saint Mary's was already a stretch for the quiet giver.

Peter did accept—and was proud of—being named an Honorary Member of the Saint Mary's Medical Staff by the doctors themselves. And he was honored to join Dr. Harold Bowman as the first two recipients of the Frank Doran, M.D., Distinguished Service Award.

The American Cancer Center's Hope Lodge, a guest home for out-of-town cancer patients and their families, is named for Peter Martin and Sophie Wege whose portrait hangs in the lobby.

In October 2005, the American Cancer Center broke ground for the first "Hope Lodge" in Michigan, a free residence for out-of-town cancer patients and their families. With the lead gift of $1 million plus $300,000 in furniture, Peter Wege and The Wege Foundation named it the Peter M. Wege Guest House after his father, Peter Martin Wege, and mother, Sophia Louise. A portrait of Peter's parents hangs in the lobby of the Hope Lodge to commemorate the dedication.

This first Hope Lodge in Michigan opened in January 2008. The $8.6 million residence has 20 suites and four communal kitchens able to house 600 cancer patients with their caregivers over a year's time. And to no one's surprise, Hope Lodge won LEED Certification from the U.S. Green Building Council.

Peter M. Wege and The Wege Foundation had one more significant gift for Peter's beloved Saint Mary's, now named Saint Mary's Medical Center. In 2012 Sophia's House opened—like Hope Lodge—to house families of hospitalized patients who live out of town. The comfortable residence is named for Sophia Dubridge Wege, mother of the lead sponsor Peter M. Wege.

On the wall in the main room hangs a picture of Peter as a young boy with his mother that reads, "This guest house is named for the woman Peter Melvin Wege referred to as 'my sainted mother.'"

In one sentence, Phil McCorkle wrapped up what Peter Wege had meant to Saint Mary's. "He is both our leader behind the scenes and our guardian angel." The man's leadership, vision, and generosity were not the only things Phil McCorkle cherished about Peter Wege. "And his jokes are legendary!"

Sophia's House named after Peter Wege's Mother, Sophia Dubridge Wege.

CHAPTER NINETEEN

THE WEGE FOUNDATION AND THE ARTS—GRAM NOT WAM

"THEN I WON'T GIVE YOU ANOTHER DIME."
PETER M. WEGE TO THE GRAND RAPIDS ART MUSEUM BOARD.

If the founding cause of The Wege Foundation in 1967 was the environment, it didn't take Peter Wege long to expand his philanthropy into education, health care, and the arts. And Peter Wege's support of his hometown's cultural life did not begin peacefully!

His earliest artistic move happened in 1969, the same year Americans landed on the moon. In the midst of setting up The Wege Foundation and starting the Center for Environmental Study, Peter still found time to co-chair a committee commissioning a major sculpture for the outdoor entryway into the city-county complex at Vandenberg Plaza in the heart of the city.

This noble cause fast became a major controversy when the committee chose the modernist French sculptor Alexander Calder to create it. Many conservative West Michigan residents disapproved calling Calder's colorful stabiles "too abstract." But Peter Wege never minded making waves if he believed in the cause. Wege enthusiastically supported the Calder commission and then helped pay for the stabile the artist created.

It didn't take long for the bright red *La Grande Vitesse*—French for "the great waters" or 'Grand Rapids'—to become the most popular artwork in town. And before long, it became the city's logo and the city center's courtyard where it stands is now renamed for it, Calder Plaza.

Peter Wege originally joined the Grand Rapids Art Museum Board as a liaison for Steelcase when it was on Fulton Street. He would go on to support the Grand Rapids Symphony, Grand Rapids Ballet, Opera Grand Rapids, St. Cecilia Music Center (St. Cecilia Music Society until 2007), and both Aquinas and the DeVos Performing Arts Centers, among other cultural organizations.

In 1969, he'd made his first donation to GRAM with a $1,000 gift beginning a lifetime of generosity to the Grand Rapids Art Museum. Indeed, when he died in 2014, Peter Wege was the Grand Rapids Art Museum's most generous patron.

He made small, but practical donations like a climate-controlled art truck and a new kitchen. He funded major exhibits—from the *Frank Lloyd Wright Light Screens* to *Masters of German Expressionism*. And Peter was especially proud to sponsor local artists like the late Mathias Alten and distinguished painter Jon MacDonald.

From 1969 into 2005, GRAM's annual donations under the name "Wege," both personal and from The Wege Foundation, have a repetitive ring. "Annual fund." "Endowment." "Underwriting." "Capital improvements."

Peter M. Wege speaking in 1969 at the unveiling of Alexander Calder's La Grande Vitesse, at the time a controversial sculpture considered too abstract.

Wege also donated his David Roberts lithograph collection that led to the naming of the main gallery. And while not his biggest, one of his favorite gifts to GRAM was an internship named for his mother the Sophia Louise Dubridge Scholarship for a college student to study in the curatorial and education departments of the Art Museum.

On September 27, 2000, Wege brought his friend former U.S. Senator Allen Simpson from Wyoming to GRAM, then located in the former Federal Court House, to open the "Unending Frontier: Art of the West." The exhibit included valuable pieces of Western art from local collectors, including Wege and his friend Peter Cook.

In 2001 The Wege Foundation announced its largest single gift and not an environmental cause, but to a cultural institution. Wege pledged $20 million for a new Grand Rapids Art Museum. His one stipulation: it had to be built according to U.S.Green Building Council LEED standards.

Still in shock at the size of Peter's generosity, the GRAM Board quickly voted to rename it the Peter Wege Art Museum. Peter's response typified his philanthropy. "Then I won't give you a dime," he told the Board. "This art museum belongs to the people of Grand Rapids, not the Wege family, and that's how the name will stay."

To make his point about who owned it, Wege insisted it be built in the heart of the city, walkable for its residents. Today, with GRAM's front doors opening to Rosa Park Circle and its year-round excitement of musicians, dancers, ice skating, and Christmas tree lightings, GRAM, indeed, belongs to the people of Grand Rapids. Just as Peter wanted it.

While this historic gift falls into The Wege Foundation's "cultural arts" mission, it also incorporates the others. The building itself is a testimony to environmental architecture; education is one of GRAM's primary activities; and, in terms of holistic health, Wege knew the opportunity to engage in the fine arts is a rich form of spiritual growth and renewal.

At the November, 2001 press conference announcing his gift to GRAM, Peter said, "My wish is that true art in all its forms should lift the mind and spirit into the realization that art can, and should be, an educational experience of huge proportions." As a boost to the future GRAM, in 2006 Peter Wege gave over $1 million to renovate the nearby 125-year-old Peninsular Club to keep bringing people downtown.

On a snowy Sunday afternoon on February 19, 2007, the first event ever held in the new $75 million Art Museum honored Peter's 87th birthday. His family and friends were awed by the world's first LEED Gold museum that proved to be a work of art in itself.

The Grand Rapids Art Museum, the first LEED certified museum in the world.

With an initial plan by London-based architects Munkenbeck & Marshall, the final building design was completed by wHY Architecture, Los Angeles, under the direction of architect Kulapat Yantrasast. Compared to the art museum in the Federal Building, the new GRAM has three times the gallery space—from 6,000 to 18,000 square feet. As one news article described it, the new GRAM is "a cultural beacon and a civic anchor." Peter Wege's vision fulfilled.

Not until this book was published did the people of Grand Rapids find out that this art museum in the heart of the city could easily have been the Wege Art Museum. But instead it is, and will remain what he wanted it to be: The Grand Rapids Art Museum.

If Peter Wege's biggest donations to the arts went to GRAM, his generosity to great music wasn't far behind. For half a century, Peter Wege proved to be one of the Grand Rapids Symphony Orchestra's best friends. As former GRSO president Melia Tourangeau put it, "Peter Wege has given to our annual fund as a major donor for as long as we have records." In one stretch alone—from 1998 to early 2005—The Wege Foundation donated $4.5 million to the Grand Rapids Symphony.

Always thinking long-term, Peter Wege and The Wege Foundation included in that sum a $2.3 million endowment gift to help ensure income for the orchestra in the future. The Wege donation helped move some of the orchestra's talented musicians from part-time to full-time positions, a transition started by the DeVos family in the 1970s. This "Music for Life" campaign also contributed to their pensions, a cause Peter gave to for many years.

"Peter has always been a champion of the musicians themselves and has always wanted them to be taken care of," Tourangeau said.

The Wege Foundation also sponsored the Grand Rapids Symphony's biennial Bravo Awards honoring community members who support the Symphony. To no one's surprise, in 1999 Peter Wege was named one of the prestigious winners. For the Bravo concert that year, the Symphony played, what else, but "Peter and the Wolf," narrated by, who else, but Peter Wege.

Portraits of Peter M. Wege drawn by young art students at the GRAM.

CHAPTER TWENTY

ART. MUSIC. DANCE. THEATER.

> "HEARING OUR SYMPHONY PLAY IN CARNEGIE HALL WAS ONE OF THE GREATEST HIGHLIGHTS OF MY LIFE."
> PETER WEGE

Peter began funding a chair named for his friend Associate Conductor John Varineau in 1997. The two men thrived on humor, and part of their fun was that John called him "Dad" while Peter called the conductor "Son." In 1999 Peter sponsored a GRSO CD featuring local pianist Rich Ridenour with Varineau conducting. In 2001 Peter Wege's "son" John Varineau was honored for his seventeen years with the GRSO in the Varineau Roundup, a celebration supported, of course, by "Dad."

Peter and The Wege Foundation were also behind the Symphony's annual fundraising golf tournament. Conductor John Varineau helped by offering to let players use his drive on a given hole or pay him not to touch a club. Varineau raised some serious Symphony cash as players were happy not to use *any* golf shot the conductor hit.

One of Music Director David Lockington's first goals when he came to Grand Rapids in 1999 was to make the Symphony available to a broader and more diverse audience. To that end Lockington created a program called, "Young, Gifted and Black." Learning of Wege's generous history for the underserved community and the Symphony, Lockington called on Peter. The "yes" was immediate.

And the cramped Symphony's administration offices on Louis Campau Promenade were furnished by Peter Wege's family business Steelcase in new roomier space at 300 Ottawa.

On October 25, 2004, Peter and The Foundation sponsored the 75th Anniversary concert called the Kathleen Battle Gala for an historic purpose. The Symphony had been invited to perform in the nation's preeminent Carnegie Hall. Getting the musicians there and housing them was not in the GRSO's budget. At the end of the Kathleen Battle Gala, the Symphony had a fresh $1 million to make Carnegie Hall happen.

On May 21, 2005, from his box seat at Carnegie Hall, Peter Wege was the first one on his feet to applaud violinist Dylana Jenson's concerto and again for the standing ovation after the concert's closing notes. "Hearing our symphony play in Carnegie Hall," Peter told David Lockington afterward, "was one of the greatest highlights of my life."

The Wege Foundation and its founder were not done with Symphony excitement. In 1999 Peter Wege heard a dynamic harpist named Deborah Henson-Conant give a Picnic Pops concert that brought the outdoor crowd to its feet. With her rainbow-ribboned curls and rock-star voice, the gifted harpist got Peter Wege's attention.

The Grand Rapids Ballet's Nutcracker Suite recreated from the children's book *Polar Express* by Grand Rapids native Chris Van Allsburg who also designed the settings.

The talented musician, described by the *Boston Globe* as a mix of "Leonard Bernstein, Steven Tyler, and Xena the Warrior Princess," became Peter's friend and protégé. In November 2005, with Peter's and The Wege Foundation's backing, three of her concerts were filmed for a DVD/CD titled *Invention & Alchemy*. The DVD/CD was released May 10, 2006, and soon made history.

In 2007 *Invention & Alchemy* was nominated for a GRAMMY in the best classical crossover category. The G.R. Symphony was the only American orchestra to be nominated in this class. And while not winning, the Symphony considered losing to the world famous London Symphony Orchestra a coup in itself putting it on the national stage. And the "Alchemy" DVD was broadcast on more than 30 PBS-TV stations around the country.

As Melia Tourangeau put it, "We'll always be the GRAMMY-nominated Grand Rapids Symphony. No one can take that away from us." In 2010 Peter and The Wege Foundation created the John P. Varineau Outstanding Music Education Award to honor a local music teacher.

Varineau explained its purpose: "Because the future of the Symphony and the future of music are tied to how we educate our children, Peter wanted this award to honor educators who help develop their students' excitement and love for music."

Besides his generosity to the Grand Rapids Symphony Orchestra, Wege supported the St. Cecilia Music Center, including $250,000 toward their building renovations at 24 Ransom. Once again with Peter's philanthropy, a friendship was behind his generosity to St Cecilia.

Chuck and Stella Royce, lifetime contributors to the St. Cecilia Music Center, were dear friends of Peter's. And what his friends cared about and believed in, Peter Wege did too. Only after Peter died in July 2014 did the Royces find out their friend had left their beloved St. Cecilia the single largest gift in the Music Center's 131-year history. One million dollars.

And Peter's unending call to "Educate! Educate! Educate" turned to action with his donations for scholarships to Interlochen, a children's music and fine-arts school in Northern Michigan.

Nor did Peter neglect the arts of dance and theater. Watching his four daughters grow up taking ballet lessons whetted Peter's interest in that art form. Over one six-year period alone, from 1999 to early 2005, he donated over $1.2 million to the Grand Rapids Ballet.

On September 13, 2006, Peter joined his friends Fred and Lena Meijer and Chuck and Stella Royce—all wearing white hard hats—in shoveling the first dirt for a $6.2 million addition to the Grand Rapids Ballet Company. The new building doubled the size of the Ballet building—formerly a bus garage—on Ellsworth on the south side of Grand Rapids. It was named the Peter Martin Wege Theatre to honor Peter's father and the grandfather of his ballerina daughters.

The 300-seat Peter Martin Wege Theatre allows the Grand Rapids Ballet Company, the only residential ballet company in the state, to expand its educational programs and performance schedule. And as with all capital projects Peter and The Wege Foundation supported after 1999, the new addition is a certified green building. Included in the approval from the U.S. Green Building Council is a green roof covered with the sedum that helps insulate the building and reduces noise.

The Wege Foundation also helped make it possible for the Grand Rapids Civic Theater to move out of its inadequate space on North Leonard and into a renovated former movie theater at 30 North Division. The bigger location for the Civic Theater increased attendance because the move into downtown Grand Rapids made it easier for theatergoers to attend the Civic's performances.

Art. Music. Dance. Theater. Historically, these vital cultural activities can't pay for themselves and have always had to count on friends who understand and appreciate the arts. In Grand Rapids, one of those friends with a capital "F" has been Peter M. Wege.

The city where his father started Metal Office Furniture in 1912 certainly knew what a friend to the arts the son of Peter Martin and Sophia Louise Wege had been. In 2004 the leaders of the arts community named Peter Melvin Wege winner of their highest honor, the Arts Council Art Award.

In presenting the award, Celeste Adams, Director of the Grand Rapids Art Museum, told the audience gathered on Calder Plaza that Peter Wege's "passion for the arts is driven by his belief that thriving cultural institutions are a vital component of a great city…he has merged his passion for global sustainability with his devotion to the quality of life in his own city and region."

In enumerating the "tapestry of arts" Wege had supported since the 1960s, Adams called it "as large as the sky above us. St. Cecilia Music Society, the Grand Rapids Symphony, Opera Grand Rapids, Grand Rapids Ballet, the Children's Museum, and the Art Museum.

"Peter Wege has what economists call, 'The Multiplier Effect,'" Celeste said. "He has touched everyone in this community. The world he would make for us all is as bright and strong and beautiful as his own spirit."

CHAPTER TWENTY ONE

A POSITIVE GRINGO AND A FIELD TRIP WITH FRED

"If we disregard the life-support system we live on, it will fail us in the not-so-distant future."

Peter M. Wege,
Economicology: The Eleventh Commandment.

From the July day in 1967 when he signed the papers creating The Wege Foundation, Peter Wege's hopes for it were broad, but focused on Grand Rapids, Michigan. It was his home for 94 years, and where all his seven children were born. But even more important was the fact his father Peter Martin Wege had moved to Grand Rapids at age 42 with patents in his pocket and a dream.

It was this city on the Grand River where his entrepreneur father had founded Metal Office Furniture—now Steelcase—and made his fortune. Forever after, his only child, Peter Melvin Wege, would see Grand Rapids as the source of his father's financial success without which there would be no Wege Foundation. Peter Wege wanted his father's assets returned to the community that had made his wealth possible. He also knew it was what both his parents would want.

Just such an opportunity came up in the early 1990s. Peter's friend and fellow philanthropist Fred Meijer asked him to support a dream he and his wife Lena had to build a world-class botanical gardens and sculpture park for Grand Rapids.

Today a visitor to Meijer Gardens can find an oversized color photograph of Fred and Peter taken in 1993 with both men wearing work shirts standing in an empty cornfield. Knowing they shared a love of nature and the outdoors, Fred had invited Peter to walk the land destined to be the Gardens. Fred also knew he and his friend Peter liked to think big about the future.

After this "field trip" with Fred, Peter didn't hesitate to support his friend's vision for a botanical and sculpture park. Today the former cornfield is Michigan's second most visited cultural destination.

David Hooker, president and CEO of Meijer Gardens, summarized the photo's meaning, "Early on, Peter Wege believed in dreams—Fred Meijer's dreams—of what would become this great institution, and his support never diminished."

Wege donated funds for the first Meijer Gardens library that Fred insisted on naming the Peter M. Wege Library. Wege also sponsored a bronze sculpture called the Book Tower in front of the library, and the Wege Nature Trail leading visitors into the Gardens' woodlands.

From Fred's first ask, The Wege Foundation has continued to say "yes" to supporting the Gardens' spectacular growth. By its tenth anniversary in 2005, the Meijer Gardens and Sculpture Park had become Michigan's second largest cultural attraction with 600,000 visitors a year.

Friends and fellow philanthropists Peter M. Wege and Fred Meijer meet in the field that became Meijer Gardens, seen below.

It wasn't the last time Peter Wege would demonstrate his friendship for the Meijer family. In 2004 Wege pledged half a million dollars toward building the West Michigan Heart Center, a world-class heart hospital named for Fred and Lena Meijer.

As Wege made his first donation to Meijer Gardens in the early 1990s, he also gave to John Ball Zoo on the west side of the Grand River where his mother Sophia Dubridge had grown up. Wege's original $300,000 gift to the city's zoo was an environmental statement as the upgrades expanded the animals' surroundings and made them better resemble their native habitats.

In 2012, Peter and The Wege Foundation again stepped up for the zoo, this time to expand the landlocked facility by installing a red trolley to carry visitors up a hill reaching formerly empty land. The funicular opened up 11 acres where guests can view the city from an observation deck. The new hilltop space also has a "tree" house that gets rented for private parties. Indeed the Bissell Tree House soon became such a popular place for weddings that brides have to sign up a year in advance.

The Meeting Hall at Camp Blodgett was a cause dear to Peter's heart because his mother Sophia was an active member of Babies Welfare Guild that continues to support the outdoor camp for underprivileged children.

In 1918 Camp Blodgett opened on Lake Michigan as a summer outdoor camp for "homeless and motherless children." The newly married Sophia Wege became one of the early members of the Babies Welfare Guild that supported the camp for underprivileged children. In addition to her financial support, Sophia Wege opened her large Lake Drive home for the Guild's yearly fundraisers.

In 2001 Peter Wege carried on his mother's favorite cause with a $100,000 gift to Camp Blodgett for a Meeting Hall on the 40-acre Lake Michigan camp property.

Since 1967, Peter Wege and The Wege Foundation have concentrated their giving locally with one notable exception. Peter's 1986 trip to Costa Rica with the Center for Environmental Study had introduced him to cutting-edge land conservation in the small Central American democracy. On that trip the country's visionary leaders President Oscar Arias and Minister Alvaro Umana convinced Wege that Costa Rica needed to be his one major international mission.

An energetic University of Pennsylvania biology professor and his scientist wife would soon confirm that judgment. Dr. Dan Janzen and Dr. Winnie Hallwachs, who spend six months a year in Costa Rica doing conservation work, entered Peter Wege's life in 1991. But Dr. Janzen had already heard about Wege from President Arias and Minister Alvaro Umana.

"His name came up frequently in the late '80s," Janzen later recalled. "They said he was one of those very positive gringos who had resources and was willing to use them to help the environment—a rarity."

Dr. Dan Janzen, a distinguished and published biology professor, and Peter Wege met in Grand Rapids in 1991 when Janzen spoke at a symposium on saving Costa Rican rain forests. What shocked the audience and impressed Peter was Janzen's radical assertion that rain forests denuded by lumbering could be restored. At the time, scientists focused on preserving uncut rain forests, believing it was too late to save those already stripped of trees.

Meijer Garden's most popular photo venue for visitors where they sit on the bench beside the bronze sculptures of Fred and Lena Meijer.

To prove reforestation can work, Dr. Janzen wanted to start in the dry forest part of the Área de Conservación Guanacaste (ACG) in northwest Costa Rica. But he needed a benefactor with long-term environmental vision. He found him in Peter Wege.

Over the next fifteen years, The Wege Foundation contributed $2.1 million to help Janzen and the Costa Rican government buy land in the ACG from private owners and then stop the burning, hunting, and logging so the forest could regrow.

While The Wege Foundation is the single biggest funder, there are 13,500 other donors—including the country of Sweden—who have collectively expanded the ACG parcel by parcel. By 2015, the ACG had grown to 414,000 acres making it a remarkable 12 percent of all Costa Rica's permanently preserved parks, wildlife refuges, biological reserves and forests.

The Wege Foundation helped guarantee continued land preservation by funding the hiring of the ACG's first executive director, Eric S. Paola, a former National Wildlife Federation executive, who now heads the Guanacaste Dry Forest Conservation Fund, to carry on ACG's environmental success story.

Thanks to the collaboration of the forward-thinking Costa Rican government, the brilliant conservationists Dr. Janzen, Dr. Hallwachs and the visionary Peter Wege, the Área de Conservación Guanacaste is now the global poster child for tropical forest restoration. The statistics prove its irreplaceable value as the ACG conserves 4 percent of the world's biodiversity and is home to 235,000 species—as many species as exist in the entire eastern half of North America!

True to The Wege Foundation's emphasis on education, every year 2,500 Costa Rican 4th-6th graders visit the ACG to study the forest's biology learning its value to their own lives. Similarly, The Wege Foundation's support has helped hire and train parataxonomists to lead the investigation and identification of the ACG's biological wealth.

Husband-and-wife team Dr. Dan Janzen and Dr. Winnie Hallwachs introduced Peter and The Wege Foundation to the mission of conserving rain and dry forests in Costa Rica.

Dr. Janzen is determined to identify every insect and plant in the ACG because, as he puts it, "If you can't name it, you won't care about it. And if you don't care about it, you won't protect it."

Talking about what The Wege Foundation's support has meant to his conservation efforts, Dr. Janzen said, "Peter Wege has been the number-one, private-sector donor in understanding, dollar support, and just plain giving us the freedom to make it happen…he has given us the economic power—and belief in us—to actually carry it out."

Not surprisingly, Peter refused to have his name attached to any of his rain-forest grants. But the wily biologist managed to outmaneuver Wege. When Dr. Janzen discovered a new species of butterfly living in the forest Peter's support had saved, the research biologist had the right to name it. This newly discovered butterfly is forever listed by the scientific name of Porphyrogenes peterwegei.

Thousands of miles south of Grand Rapids, a delicate butterfly flits through a lush piece of Guanacaste rain forest honoring the man who helped preserve them both.

CHAPTER TWENTY TWO

GO BLUE, THINK GREEN AND EARTH UNIVERSITY

"WE WERE VERY GRATEFUL PETER ACCEPTED OUR INVITATION."

DR. JONATHAN BULKLEY, UNIVERSITY OF MICHIGAN
SCHOOL OF NATURAL RESOURCES AND ENVIRONMENT.

Peter Wege's enthusiasm for Dr. Janzen's conservation work in Costa Rica wasn't The Wege Foundation's only love affair with the small Central American country. If reforesting the Guanacaste had seemed an impossible dream, so did a wild idea called EARTH University.

By the 1980s, scientists recognized the vital diversity of life in Costa Rica's rainforests was threatened by lumbering, ranching, and destructive farming. In 1986 a collaboration of visionary thinkers from both the government and private sector took a leap of faith to do something about it.

The first college of its kind in the world, EARTH University opened in 1990 in the middle of the Costa Rican rainforest. It fulfilled the dream of its first president Jose A. Zaglu to educate young Latin Americans on sustainable agriculture. The long-term goal was for EARTH University's graduates to return to their home communities in Central and South America where they would teach their fellow farmers how to raise crops using sustainable methods.

Victor Sanchez, with EARTH University Foundation, recalled the day Peter Wege first visited the school in June 1991 having been invited by Dr. Russell Mawby and Dr. Norman Brown from the W.K. Kellogg Foundation. "Dr. Mawby and Dr. Brown knew Peter's long history of environmental activism," Sanchez said. "They also knew he loved young people and had always supported education."

The Kellogg Foundation leaders were right. When Wege met the enthusiastic President Jose A. Zaglul and saw what was happening at EARTH University with its 8,000-acre farm bordering a rainforest preserve, he "got very excited," Sanchez recalled.

With half of EARTH University's students too poor to pay tuition, The Wege Foundation began funding scholarships—and never stopped. Sanchez explained, "We tell the students, 'This scholarship is not for you; it's for the community you come from.'"

In 2005 after 994 men and women had graduated from EARTH University, 92 percent remained in Latin America; 77 percent back in their home communities. And by 2005 the freshman class was 42 percent female because the first women graduates went home and recruited other females to apply to EARTH University. By 2009, EARTH University, with its rigorous four-year, six-days a week, year-round curriculum had some 1,500 alums from 25 different nations.

Central and South American college students at EARTH University in Costa Rica. At his tuition-free school, the students learn sustainable farming methods they then take home to teach other farmers.

A sign of its global recognition is the fact that Whole Foods buys its bananas from EARTH University knowing they use organic fertilizer, reuse 30 percent of their water, plant ground cover to protect the soil, and even reuse the blue banana bags and pallets to make wastebaskets.

How did Peter Wege's early involvement affect this remarkably successful mission of educating a new generation of Latin Americans on sustainable agriculture? Victor Sanchez, from EARTH University's Foundation, said of those early years in the 1990s, "Peter gave us immediate credibility…The Wege Foundation fast-forwarded the University."

Wege visited EARTH U five times, always keeping a low profile, according to Sanchez. But the students loved it when he came and they admired his vigor. "Peter had great fun talking to them…he was a voice of inspiration to these kids."

From Sanchez's perspective, the environmental impact of The Wege Foundation's support for EARTH University extends far beyond Costa Rica's borders. "Peter Wege has made a difference in this hemisphere," Sanchez said simply.

Back in the USA, on October 28, 2004, Peter Wege spoke to 200 University of Michigan freshmen in the School of Natural Resources and the Environment (SNRE). As he hiked up and down the lecture room's steps answering students' keen questions about economicology, Wege's enthusiasm won the students over.

It had all started with a lunch at the Holiday Inn in Lansing, Michigan, thirteen years earlier.

Monday, December 9, 1991, three passionate environmentalists, two driving west from Ann Arbor and one driving east from Grand Rapids, sat down for lunch at the Holiday Inn in Lansing.

Dr. Jonathan Bulkley, an international expert on water and a faculty member at the SNRE, Dr. Greg Keoleian, a post-doctoral Fellow at SNRE, and Peter Wege met for the first time near the Michigan State University campus.

The fact that these three Michigan men entered each others' lives at MSU gives added flavor to one of Wege's most repeated wisdoms: Go Blue, Think Green.

The year before their Holiday Inn lunch, Greg Keoleian had spent time at Steelcase doing research on private businesses that practiced pollution prevention because the Grand Rapids company was known as a pioneering environmental manufacturer. Then Dr. Keoleian's Steelcase guide happened to hand him a copy of the company's latest newsletter.

That's where the research scientist saw an article about a Steelcase executive named Peter Wege who had pushed his company toward green manufacturing. Keoleian realized it was Wege's leadership that helped initiate Steelcase's creative, recyclable packaging.

Back in Ann Arbor, Keoleian wrote up his case study on Steelcase, and tucked the newsletter away in, appropriately, a Steelcase file cabinet. Keoleian would later learn that it was Peter Wege's father who'd invented the rollers that made the SNRE's long file drawers possible!

In 1991, the year after Keoleian's Steelcase tour, the U.S. Environmental Protection Agency published a national request for proposal in the Federal Register asking for applications from colleges and universities to host a new Pollution Prevention Center.

Jonathan Bulkley and Greg Keoleian couldn't resist. Along with 27 other schools across the country, they submitted a preliminary proposal. After reviewing all 28 entries, the EPA asked six of the colleges to send in final grant proposals. Out of the six finalists, one would be chosen as the National Pollution Prevention Center for Higher Education. And the winner was…

The University of Michigan's School of Natural Resources and the Environment created the nation's first Pollution Prevention Center. Once Jonathan and Greg were done celebrating, they went to work meeting the grant's specific requirements. One of EPA's mandates was to create an External Advisory Board to be composed of leading individuals from industry, government, and non-governmental organizations.

After finding highly qualified people to sit on the new board, Dr. Jonathan Bulkley told Greg they still needed a chairman. That's when Dr. Keoleian remembered the Steelcase article and retrieved it from his file. The two academicians quickly concluded Peter Wege looked like the perfect candidate to become the National Pollution Prevention Center's first advisory board chair.

At the Holiday Inn December 9, 1991, Peter heard how crucial the advisory board would be to the NPPC's success and said he would talk it over with his family. Then, with his family's encouragement, Wege agreed to represent Steelcase as the first chairperson of the External Advisory Board for the new Pollution Prevention Center at the school where'd he'd set a javelin record.

Dr. Bulkley would later say, "We were very grateful Peter accepted our invitation." Busy as he already was, chairing such a board perfectly matched Peter's earliest dreams for The Wege Foundation. As Peter later wrote in one of his economicology essays, "What I have said and done and talked about since the beginning is clean air, clean water, and a healthy way to dispose of waste."

CHAPTER TWENTY THREE

POPULAR ANNUAL WEGE LECTURES AT U OF M AND AQUINAS

"ONCE AGAIN WE'RE ROBBING PETER TO PAY PAUL."
AQUINAS COLLEGE PRESIDENT PAUL NELSON ON PETER WEGE'S
AND THE WEGE FOUNDATION'S ONGOING GIFTS TO THE SCHOOL.

In 1997, six years after the National Pollution Prevention Center was founded, its external board chaired by Peter Wege moved to the next level supporting Bulkley's and Keoleian's plan for the NPPC to evolve into a new Center for Sustainable Systems. Expanding it to 'sustainability' was a logical progression reaching beyond just preventing pollution.

While sustainability has become the driving force of the environmental movement, it is defined in different ways. The one most widely repeated comes from the World Commission on Environment and Development: "Meeting the needs of the present without compromising the ability of future generations to meet their own needs."

Pioneering green architect William McDonough explains sustainability in terms of design: "Sustainable design is the conception and realization of ecologically, economically, and ethically responsible expression as a part of the evolving matrix of nature."

If chairing the board for the first National Pollution Prevention Center was Peter Wege's first collaboration with the University of Michigan, it wasn't his last. Over the next 15 years, Peter Wege and Jonathan Bulkley would team up time and again in academic-environmental partnerships.

Ellen Satterlee, President of the Wege Foundation, explained why Peter and Dr. Bulkley connected so fast and became such good friends: "Jonathan Bulkley embraced Peter's passion and understanding for the environment in his own quiet and gentle way. Jonathan is a man of high integrity and subtle persuasion. He is an example of the way The Wege Foundation works."

Among other gifts, The Wege Foundation sponsored several of the CSS's research projects, including a study on preventing pollution on cruise ships. Another grant supported the University of Michigan's participation in a national environmental survey of colleges and universities. In addition, The Wege Foundation funds a scholarship for students from the University of Michigan's School of Natural Resources to work as interns at Steelcase.

One of The Wege Foundation's largest gifts to the University of Michigan's School of Natural Resources and the Environment was a $1.5 million grant over three years for an endowed chair. Peter was delighted when the Regents named his friend Professor Jonathan W. Bulkley the first faculty member to hold the Peter M. Wege Chair of Sustainable Systems.

An ongoing bonus of Wege's generosity to Michigan is the annual lecture the University insisted on naming in his honor. The first

Peter M. Wege Lecture on October 17, 2001, was given by the new dean of the SNRE, Dr. Rosina M. Bierbaum, an international authority on global climate change. Dr. Joseph Sax, a pioneer in environmental law, delivered the 2002 Peter M. Wege lecture, "Reflections on the Great Lakes."

In 2004, Dr. Peter Newman, a professor from Murdoch University in Australia, spoke on "Cities as Sustainable Ecosystems." Gro Harlem Bruntland, three-time Prime Minister of Norway and former Director of the World Health Organization, spoke in 2004 on "Sustainable Development—A Global Perspective on Ecology, Economy & Equity."

In 2005 The University of Michigan Alumni Magazine published a picture of Peter Wege with the keynote speaker for the 5th annual lecture series, Al Gore, the 45th Vice-President of the United States. Gore, a dedicated environmentalist who'd lost his bid for the Presidency to George W. Bush in a recount the year before, spoke on "Global Climate Change."

In 2007, William Clay Ford, Jr., Executive Chairman of Ford Motor Company, delivered the Seventh Annual Peter M. Wege Lecture titled, "The Road To Sustainable Transportation."

Through the 1990s, the University of Michigan was not the only college blessed by Peter's passion for education. Facing a financial crisis in the early 1990s, Aquinas College inevitably turned to its most generous friend. As always, Peter Wege, co-chairman of the school's Board of Trustees at the time, answered the need.

In 1995 The Wege Foundation gave Aquinas $5 million— the largest gift in the school's history, and the second largest ever given to any college in Grand Rapids. Indeed, while Paul Nelson served as Aquinas president from 1990 to 1997, he had a favorite saying. "Once again," President Nelson would quip about Wege's ongoing donations to the college, "we're robbing Peter to pay Paul!"

In 1997, Wege joined forces with Clare F. Jarecki, another generous Aquinas friend, to create the Jarecki School for Advanced Learning. The new school's mission was to create working interactions between local businesses and the academia of Aquinas College. The Jarecki School thus dovetailed into Peter Wege's advocacy for both education and collaboration.

Wege guaranteed that economicology would be part of the Jarecki program when he donated solar panels for the new

Vice-President Al Gore greets Peter M. Wege after delivering the 2005 Peter M. Wege Lecture at the University of Michigan titled, "Global Climate Change."

Economicology gathering at Aquinas College in April 2006.

building's roof. Business leaders meeting in the highly computerized, fully wired building would experience first-hand how much energy—fuel costs—could be saved by drawing on the free power of the sun's rays.

But the solar power hadn't been a slam dunk. The head of facilities for Aquinas at the time, Tom Summers recalled the 1997 planning meeting when Wege first proposed photovoltaic panels on the Jarecki Center's roof.

Tom Summers was skeptical. "As a facilities person," he later told a *Press* reporter, "Does the dang thing work? I had to wonder. And will the roof leak?'" Tom Summers recalled his astonishment when the Jarecki solar panels started producing power even as they were unloaded from the truck.

Seven years after the Jarecki Center went up, Summers sounded like Peter in his enthusiasm for the sun's energy coming from the roof of Aquinas's newly renovated field house with its 6,000 square feet of solar panels. "It just keeps running," Summers said. "It has been fantastic."

Peter Wege continued his bond with Aquinas in 1997 when he hosted his first annual lecture on campus addressing issues relevant to both economicology and human spirituality. The Wege Speaker Series soon became a popular April event. Typifying the quality of speakers, Robert F. Kennedy, Jr., son of the late Senator Robert F. Kennedy, gave the 2001 lecture.

With his distinct Kennedy looks, this environmental lawyer talked about his collaboration with angry fishermen and conservationists to successfully prosecute several major corporations for polluting the Hudson River. The fishermen's unprecedented victory in the New York court led to a national movement called "The Riverkeepers," volunteers who patrol rivers around the country looking for destructive runoff entering the water. If they discover any, the polluters have to stop what they're doing and pay to clean the water.

The Wege Speaker Series takes place in Aquinas College's Performing Arts Center, the elegant, high-tech auditorium that Peter Wege helped build in 2003 replacing the 250-seat Kretschmer Hall. Peter Wege had also helped pay for Kretschmer when it was built.

The new PAC was the product of vintage Wege collaboration. Aquinas needed a performing arts auditorium, and Grand Rapids Circle Theatre needed to move out of its dated facility at John Ball Zoo. Presto! Aquinas's performing-arts people met with those from Civic Theatre and jointly planned the acoustically sophisticated auditorium now home to them both.

And the collaboration expanded. Catholic Central and West Catholic high schools needed a stage for their arts performances, and the new PAC became their auditorium as well.

To no one's surprise, when Aquinas College created the Reflections Award to honor friends of the school, Peter M. Wege was named one of the first winners in 1998. In 2002, eighty years after the college was founded, Peter Wege was elected to Aquinas College's Hall of Fame.

In 1998, the Council of Michigan Foundations named Peter Wege the Honorary Chair of its annual conference. CMF's speaker at that Lansing conference honoring Wege was South Africa's revered Archbishop Desmond Tutu who talked about the end of apartheid.

Peter M. Wege being honored by Aquinas College's Reflections Award and receiving congratulations from his good friend Ralph Hauenstein.

CHAPTER TWENTY FOUR

FATHER MARK, LOWELL, AND THE NATURE CONSERVANCY

"In this book, I am drawing on the best minds who have written on this subject in my overpowering wish to wake up my fellow citizens while there's still time."

Peter M. Wege,
Economicology: The Eleventh Commandment.

In 1975, the Aquinas Alumni Association had given Peter Wege its Outstanding Service Award. Sixteen years later in 1991, Wege was named winner of Aquinas's Emeritus Award honoring a person "whose dedication to the welfare of all citizens serves as a light to guide those who follow."

In the Emeritus Award ceremonies, Aquinas College president Paul Nelson described Wege as "an industrialist, ecologist, environmentalist, futurist, and supporter of causes for human betterment" as well as a "staunch and loyal friend" of Aquinas.

In his acceptance speech, Wege called for creating greater understanding among all the planet's inhabitants because "we are a global family" and thus inter-connected. He spoke on the need to educate world leaders about the major environmental dangers, starting with overpopulation, chemical hazards, and global warming.

The highlight of the 1991 Emeritus Award evening for Peter Wege was introducing his two beloved St. Stephen's grade school teachers: Sister Mary Leonard, his kindergarten teacher in 1926, and Sister Vincent DePaul, who'd taught him in fifth, sixth, and seventh grades. Wege never forgot what he owed to those good sisters and his solid Catholic education.

When the St. Stephen's priest Father Mark Przybysz came to Grand Rapids in the summer of 1995, he was given the name of that parish's best friend. It didn't take long for Father Mark to invite Peter Wege for lunch. This meeting certainly proved there is no such thing as a free lunch! Father Mark's new parish and its school faced a $65,000 debt and outdated technology.

But as happened often with Peter Wege, Father Mark didn't have to ask. Peter's first question to his new priest was, "Now what can I do to help?"

Father Mark recalled: "I told him of the debt, and he said, 'What else?' I told him we needed new computers for the offices." Without pause, Wege gave St. Stephen $100,000 and another $25,000 if his fellow parishioners would match it.

Grateful as Father Mark was for Wege's quick generosity, he was not eager to begin his ministry by asking his congregation for the matching $25,000. But when Father Mark announced Wege's offer from the pulpit, it took only two weeks for St. Stephen's members to more than match by pledging $33,000.

Four years later, Wege once again gave back to what had been given to him as a young boy at St. Stephen's School. An unusable

Peter M. Wege with his friend and priest Father Mark Przybysz.

section of the basement held the possibility of more classroom space the school badly needed. Peter Wege agreed to pay for the major renovation Father Mark described as "a welcome needed addition" for the school and religious education.

When Father Mark offered him the naming privilege, Peter refused. But then he thought about all his mother had done to help St. Stephen's School get started. He relented, in his typical way, by naming it for Sophia Dubridge Wege.

In 2003, the Catholic diocese moved Father Mark from Peter's neighborhood parish at St. Stephen's across town to St. Anthony's in northwest Grand Rapids. Despite the longer drive, Wege followed Father Mark to his new church.

From their first "no free lunch" in 1995 until Peter died July 7, 2014, Father Mark was Peter's priest and close friend. Over the last two years of Peter's declining health, the outgoing Father Mark visited him regularly, both to pray with his friend and to make him laugh.

After conducting the service and mass at Peter's funeral July 11, 2014, Father Mark asked everyone in the packed Cathedral of Saint Andrew to come outside for a final farewell. "We can't say goodbye to Peter Wege indoors," he said vigorously.

Outside in the sun surrounded by mourners, Father Mark stood on the Secchia compass embedded on the Cathedral's plaza and began pointing his finger and turning. In each direction, Father Mark called out the good works Peter had done located where he was pointing. It took some time for Peter's friend and priest to complete his 360-degree circle.

And everyone gathered to honor Peter—family and friends— knew what Father Mark was doing. Naming only some of the ways Peter M. Wege had made his hometown a better place to live. If he'd named them all, they would have been standing in the July heat for a very long time.

Peter M. Wege's advice to "get the kids outdoors" and to "educate, educate, educate" is actively alive and well at Lowell's Wittenbach-Wege Environmental Center.

In 1999, school and city officials in Lowell gathered to dedicate sixty-two pristine acres of rolling land just north of Lowell High School as a permanent nature conservancy open to the public year-round. The Land Conservancy of West Michigan dedicated it to the donors as the Wittenbach-Wege Environmental Center.

This gift in Lowell underscored two of Peter Wege's lifelong missions: the environment and education. By preserving these acres of flourishing trees and wildlife near the high school, Wege knew students would visit the area. "If we're going to save the planet," Peter said about his gift, "we need to educate young people about nature right now."

Peter's vision was that the young people who came to walk in the woods would come to love the natural world—and then go on to help take care of it.

The world's largest conservation organization, The Nature Conservancy (Michigan Chapter), honored Peter Wege in April 2005 for his $1 million Leadership Gift to the biggest conservation drive in the state's history. That year the Nature Conservancy raised an unprecedented $78 million to preserve the state's most ecologically sensitive areas.

Under the Nature Conservancy's banner of saving "Michigan's Last Great Places," their 30,000 members preserved over 423 square miles in the Upper Peninsula. Included in this land across seven UP counties are 23,338 pristine acres in the Two Hearted River watershed.

Called the Northern Great Lakes Forest Project, this historic preservation of land and 25 miles of Great Lakes shoreline makes this area permanently available to the public for hiking, canoeing, fishing, and hunting. And because sustainable timber harvesting is permitted there, these Upper Peninsula woods provide lumbering jobs in the private sector. Economicology in action.

The Grand Rapids Public School's C.A. Frost Environmental Science Academy grades K-8.

In addition to conserving the U.P. land, The Wege Foundation helped the Nature Conservancy preserve a significant piece of Lake Michigan shoreline in Saugatuck. In a ceremony accepting the Nature Conservancy's appreciation for his gifts, Peter Wege told the audience, "Because Michigan holds a unique place at the center of the Great Lakes ecosystem, the work of The Nature Conservancy is incredibly important not only to the future of our state, but also for our region."

Conserving the natural environment was a high priority for Peter Wege; but his top environmental mission was to educate people, especially the young, about the glory and value of the Earth they inhabit. In 2001, The Wege Foundation gave a $1 million grant to the National Wildlife Federation for children to build wildlife habitats on their schools' playgrounds.

The children learned which flowers, shrubs, and trees attract which birds and insects. Some habitats became butterfly gardens, some rain gardens. Peter Wege attended as many of the Grand Rapids habitat plantings as he could. They gave him time with his favorite audience—young people—about his favorite cause—caring for the environment. It also gave the children the chance to thank him with cards, poems, and drawings honoring their environmental hero.

In the fall of 2005, The Wege Foundation opened a new schoolyard habitat at the C.A. Frost Environmental Science Academy. To highlight the occasion, Wege brought in TV star Jack Hanna of the popular series *Jack Hanna's Animal Adventures*.

CHAPTER TWENTY FIVE

GILDA'S CLUB AND THE DREAM-MAKER

"Why take two, When one will do?"
Stickers Peter M. Wege had distributed to be put on
public bathrooms' paper towel dispensers.

No suffering touched Peter Wege's broad capacity for the "E" of empathy more deeply than the disease of cancer. Certainly his father's dying of oral cancer in 1947 followed by his mother's death from breast cancer in 1959 made fighting that affliction personal for him.

In 1998, three breast cancer survivors, Susan Smith, Deb Bailey, and Twink Frey McKay, decided Grand Rapids needed a Gilda's Club named for the comedienne Gilda Radner who died of ovarian cancer. Created in her memory, Gilda's Clubs around the country offered a homelike atmosphere where cancer patients and their families could come together for support, education, fellowship, and fun.

Their idea started to become reality when Twink and her husband Jim McKay donated land on Bridge Street that had a 6,000 square-foot house and an unusable barn. But the founders still needed major financial help to make the club happen.

Peter Wege's name came up early in their conversations because they knew him as a man of kindness, generosity, and a willingness to help others. The future director of Gilda's Club Grand Rapids, Leann Arkema recalled the freezing January 1999 day when she and Jim McKay prepared their rehearsed pitch to Peter and Ellen Satterlee in the old farm house. As bad luck would have it, the aged boiler quit and the kitchen was freezing.

Leann described the scene, "The four of us sat huddled with our overcoats on trying to keep our hands warm over cups of hot soup I'd brought in." Then, before Jim or she had a chance to promote the Club's needs, Peter spoke up. "Well, yes, we'll help you. How much is this project going to cost?"

"Jim and I just I sat in silence because he'd thrown us off," Leann recalled, still smiling at the memory. "We hadn't said a word of what we'd planned." When she finally found her tongue, Leann was so rattled she told Wege $300,000, which wasn't even the number they'd meant to ask for, but he said 'yes' too fast to correct it. Later on Leann Arkema said about the morning of visible breaths in the cold kitchen, "That day Peter changed the entire course of history for Gilda's Club."

Wege's preemptive generosity immediately made the new 'barn' room possible. And without that extra space, Gilda's Club could not have accomplished what it so unexpectedly did. By the end of 2005, five years after opening Gilda's hallmark red front door, over 10,000 cancer families from 29 counties had come to the Club, averaging 400 visits a week.

The barn that Peter and The Wege Foundation built for the cancer support non-profit Gilda's Club painted in the Club's signature red. The garden and pool behind Gilda's Club.

Peter Melvin Wege 1920-2014

"Because of Peter's gift, we were instantly able to do what we never could have without him." The original goal in March 2001 had been to reach 200-250 visits a month. But in the second month alone, over 700 cancer patients and family members made their way through the red door on Bridge Street.

In the welcoming rebuilt barn space Peter Wege helped provide, these hurting families ate, talked, learned, shared, cried, did arts and crafts, yoga, played music and experienced the 'E' for empathy only others who've been there can give.

As fast and as gratifying as Gilda's success was, it created new problems. Because it is free to cancer families, by 2001 the Club was running short on supplies and staff. "We now had terminally ill people coming—their families were being torn apart," Leann recalls, "and we were going to have to go part-time."

Knowing they couldn't go back to the community for more funds so soon after their original capital campaign, the board, once again, turned to Peter Wege. Taking no chances on heat this time, they took Peter and Ellen to the Peninsular Club for lunch and asked for $150,000 to match a Frey Foundation grant. Peter said he'd think about it.

He did. On their way home from the Pen Club, Ellen called from the car and said Peter didn't want to give what they'd asked for. He wanted to give them $200,000. Vintage Peter Wege.

But he still wasn't done. Six months later, in the summer of 2001, Leann was showing Peter around Gilda's Club. She apologized about the tight parking. Another downside of their phenomenal success was more traffic than they'd ever envisioned. "It was only an offhand comment," Leann recalls. "Nothing more."

Gilda's Club first director Leann Arkema and Peter Wege after a Gilda's Club golf outing. Peter's golf shirt sports his ECONOMICOLOGY logo.

But Peter Wege saw a problem that needed fixing. "I want to build you another parking lot. Give Ellen the bill." Stunned as Leann was by this unasked-for gift, by now she wasn't surprised. "Peter Wege doesn't just give his money away," Arkema explained, "he cares. He's interested in you—what you're doing. He asks all the right questions. He's obviously very intelligent."

By 2001, Gilda's Club of Grand Rapids was the busiest of the 20 Clubs in the country. The original Gilda's in New York City was second at the time with 5,000 fewer visitors a year than the Grand Rapids Club. By the time Peter died in 2014, Gilda's was serving 10,000 people a year with visits and programs. Equally impressive that year were the 1,300 volunteers who served Gilda's with gratitude for the help given their families.

Gilda's Club director Leann Arkema spoke for many people when she described Peter Wege as a "dream-maker."

CHAPTER TWENTY SIX

A RIVER RESTORED, LEED GETS MANDATORY, AND KERMIT THE FROG

"We must make environmental and ecological issues as important as economics."

Peter M. Wege,
Economicology: The Eleventh Commandment.

As Grand Rapids' First Man of Environmental Activism since the 1970s, Peter M. Wege's reputation for green good works was well known beyond Grand Rapids. That's why in 1999 a small grassroots group in Muskegon knew where to go when they saw their prized, namesake river was in jeopardy. Popular for fishing with its cool water, the Muskegon River was growing too warm for trout and getting polluted as well.

But again one of Peter's friends played a major role in connecting these good people in Muskegon to The Wege Foundation. Jack Bails from the Great Lakes Fishery Trust and Peter had partnered for the environment before. Jack knew Peter would understand the threat to this great river—and he would care about it.

For The Wege Foundation, it was history come full circle. Cleaning up the Grand River had been its earliest charge when Wege set up the Center for Environmental Study. The success of those early efforts confirmed Wege's faith that communities could fight the destruction of public waters.

In August 2000, The Wege Foundation and the Great Lakes Fishery Trust sponsored a three-day conference in Muskegon where scientists from major academic institutions around the state, conservationists, and representatives from other non-profits gathered to map out a strategy for saving what the GLFT had declared a "priority watershed."

The conference led to a collaboration named the Muskegon River Watershed Assembly to fund studies that could serve as models for protecting other river watersheds around the Great Lakes.

One of MRWA's first projects was planting wild rice, bulrush, and other vegetation in Muskegon Lake to restore the habitat for fish and wildlife. On one cold November day in 2003, the volunteer planters had to break ice before they could wade into the water with their wild rice seeds!

In another MRWA project, volunteers planted the eggs and larvae of milfoil weevils in Higgins Lake to prey on the invasive aquatic-plant species Eurasian Watermilfoil. In the town of Hershey, the MRWA set in motion removal of a dilapidated dam to open the flow of water for the migration of fish and other aquatic species between the Hershey River and the Muskegon River.

In April 2001, The Wege Foundation joined the Great Lakes Fisheries Trust to hire staff so the MRWA could continue its

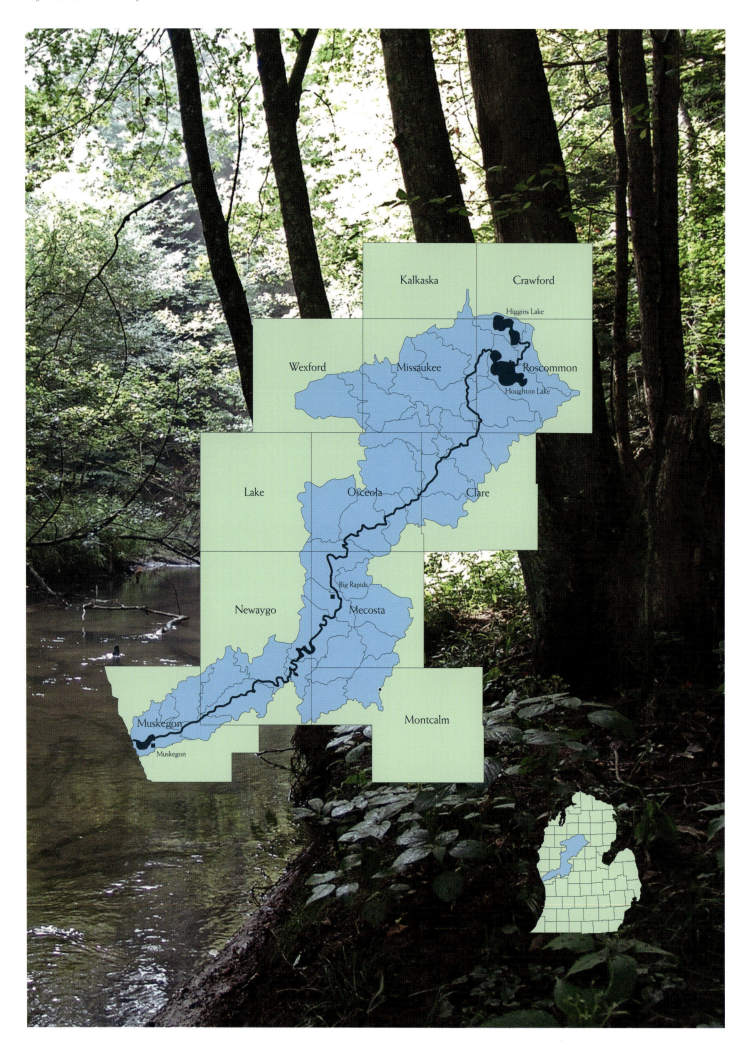

Map of the watershed surrounding the second longest river in Michigan, the Muskegon River at 216 miles.

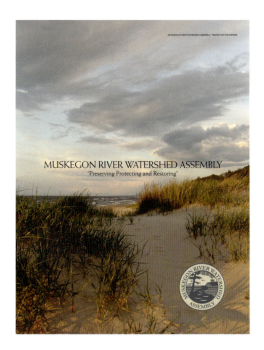

The logo and brochure for the Muskegon River Watershed Assembly.

mission of preserving, protecting, and restoring the Muskegon Watershed. Peter also offered to match donations from other funders. Always an advocate of collaboration, Wege saw this matching offer as a way to bring more supporters to the table.

Wege's gifts also helped produce the video, "The Muskegon River Initiative" that premiered at Muskegon's Beardsley Theatre in September 2003. Former State Representative Lana Pollack, at the time president of the Michigan Environmental Council, was the keynote speaker who would also become a major force in Wege's Great Lakes campaign.

Speaking to Peter's concept of economicology, Pollack noted that with 425,000 people living in the watershed of the Muskegon River, protecting the water's quality was an economic as well as an ecological necessity. "There's more money to be made in preventing pollution," Pollack told the audience, "than in restoring the water after the damage is done." She noted that the Muskegon Watershed is larger than the state of Delaware.

By the time Peter Wege died in 2014, the Hershey dam had been removed and the fish were returning to the lower Hershey River. And by 2015 the MRWA had spent over $4 million in projects from Higgins Lake to Newago restoring the ecology of the great Muskegon River.

The Wege Foundation's 2003 annual report described its five separate missions as one rich tapestry because they seamlessly weave through one another. Environment. Education. Health Care. Arts and Culture. Community Service. Yet it was the environment that first caught Wege's attention in the plane over Pittsburgh making Green stand out as the dominant color in the fabric of The Wege Foundation.

And it was one announcement in 2003 that changed forever the building landscape in Grand Rapids. Peter Wege put out the word that The Wege Foundation would no longer consider a capital gift unless the proposed construction received LEED certification through the United States Green Building Council.

In 2017 the University of Michigan's Center for Sustainable Systems was renamed the School For Environment & Sustainability.

LEED, the acronym for Leadership in Energy and Environmental Design, certification means new construction must meet specific standards of sustainability developed by the USGBC. To win the prestigious LEED certification, new buildings must earn a minimum number of environmental points.

These guidelines reaffirm Wege's principle of economicology as LEED construction saves water and energy, thus protecting both the ecology and the economy. LEED buildings also promote economicology because the indoor air is healthier and thus employees are more productive. Finally, the up-front higher construction expenses of LEED buildings are offset long-term because a green building lasts longer and costs less to run.

When Christine Ervin, the head of the USGBC, delivered the 2004 Wege Speaker Series lecture at Aquinas College, she echoed Peter Wege's vision of economicology in LEED buildings.

"The best sustainable designs are not just environmentally responsible," Ervin told the audience, "they also produce buildings where employees can thrive and productivity can soar." Ervin's lecture that day was about to make history at Habitat for Humanity

Five years before, Peter Wege and The Wege Foundation had already proved the value of LEED principles at the University of Michigan. Ann Arbor's 19th Century Dana Building housing the University's School of Natural Resources and the Environment (SNRE) needed such expensive repairs, U of M officials considered tearing it down.

But Peter Wege's good friends SNRE professors Dr. Jonathan Bulkley and Dr. Greg Keoleian urged the University instead to restore and expand Dana using LEED standards. Peter Wege was involved from the get-go in what would be known as "The Greening of Dana." The restoration of this 19th Century building won national attention as a living laboratory of environmental reconstruction.

From installing composting toilets and waterless urinals to glass tiles made from recycled airplane windshields, the Greening of Dana was a hands-on clinic for SNRE students.

Nobody was prouder of the new green Dana than Peter Wege. "The 'Greening of Dana,'" Wege was eager to tell people, "is a perfect example of what I call, 'Go Blue, Think Green.'" In 2005 the Dana Building received a gold rating from the USGBC making it the greenest academic building in Michigan.

At the same time, three thousand miles west, The Wege Foundation's gift of a 47-kilowatt photovoltaic system was going up on the roof of the Donald Bren School of Environmental Science & Management at the University of California in Santa Barbara.

In 2002, the Bren School became the second building in the country to earn a Platinum LEED rating, the highest award granted by the USGBC. In ceremonies on the University of California's Santa Barbara campus honoring Peter for his gift, Bren School's Dean Dennis Aigner thanked Wege in an unusually green way. Peter Wege got to shake "hands" with the real Kermit the Frog internationally known as the star of the Muppets—the TV show that premiered the year The Wege Foundation was created.

In dedicating the pioneering green building, the University of California's Dean Dennis Aigner endorsed economicology. "The business case for sound environmental practices is becoming more compelling every day. In the near future, a company's environmental record will be tantamount to a license to operate."

Wege's 2003 decision to fund only LEED-certified buildings had a profound affect on his hometown. By 2006, West Michigan had more LEED buildings up, or going up, than any other comparably sized area in the country.

And Peter Wege wasn't done blazing trails in green building. His next project would make national waves and it grew out of Wege's fondness and respect for his priest and friend Father Mark Przybysz.

CHAPTER TWENTY SEVEN

FOR FRIENDS: A NEW RECTORY AND A NEW LIBRARY

"ALL THE TECHNOLOGY AND COMPUTER SYSTEMS IN THE UNIVERSE WILL
NOT BE ENOUGH TO SAVE CIVILIZATION UNLESS WE HAVE THE WISDOM AND
INTELLIGENCE TO USE THEM FOR THE RIGHT PURPOSES."

PETER M. WEGE,
ECONOMICOLOGY: THE ELEVENTH COMMANDMENT.

The day in 2003 Peter Wege's friend and priest Father Mark Przybysz invited Wege to his new home in the St. Anthony's rectory, The Wege Foundation's chief saw the chance he'd been looking for. The 50-year old rectory was a mishmash of add-ons that needed radical reconstruction. When "green" remodeling turned out not to be an option, Wege offered up to $500,000 to tear down the rectory and build the first LEED-certified residence on the planet.

For Father Mark and his parishioners at St. Anthony's, good stewardship is a calling of their Catholic faith. So Peter Wege's offer was eagerly accepted. A humanitarian upgrade would be added to the stewardship piece because the new rectory would be barrier-free where the old one was not.

Hired to do the work, Rockford Construction donated enough time and material to be considered a full partner in building Peter Wege's dream LEED house. The problem was that the U.S. Green Building Council had not yet developed ratings for home construction meaning Villa Verde, the "green home," earned points using LEED commercial standards.

They began collecting points using the original foundation and recycling all the razed materials, the brick and concrete crushed to be recycled for building roads. The old doors and sliders went into affordable homes built by Habitat for Humanity.

Villa Verde's landscaping is low water, requiring no sprinklers, and the siding is made of a sawdust-cement mixture. The wood floors came from pine beams salvaged from the Durfee Building in Grand Rapids, the rugs made from recycled used carpeting. The kitchen cabinets are built from fast-growing poplar wood with compressed cardboard interiors. Created by a local artist, the rectory's signature stained-glass window tells the Villa Verde story letting in natural light.

Villa Verde became the poster residence for green-home building and was regularly toured by architects, builders, developers, and families wanting to learn how environmental houses save natural resources and are healthier with cleaner air.

In early 2007, Peter Wege gave another $1.2 million to St. Anthony's School on Richmond Street to add six classrooms and renovate the current ones for pre-school through eighth-grade. Like the parish house itself, the 7,000 square-foot expansion was built to LEED standards. Wege later added solar panels that provide more than the necessary energy to handle the expansion.

In 2009, when Peter's gift of a new wind turbine on the school's chimney was dedicated, a banner was hung across the entire front of the school reading, "Thank You Mr. Wege."

St. Anthony's was one of the first rooftop wind turbines in West Michigan. Built locally by Cascade Engineering, the Swift Wind Turbine proved the truth of Wege's economicology by reducing the electric bills and lowering the amount of carbon dioxide released.

"When the environment and education come together," Ellen Satterlee told the media at the dedication, "you have two of Mr. Wege's favorite projects."

Peter Wege and The Wege Foundation donated an identical rooftop wind turbine to GRPS's City High/Middle School, home of the economicology curriculum funded by The Wege Foundation. Each of these rooftop turbines costs between $10,000 and $12,000 installed, with at least 30 percent of that refunded in tax credits for energy savings.

"Every once in a great while you come across a prophet," Father Mark Przybysz said during the turbine's dedication at St. Anthony's. "Peter Wege is a modern-day prophet proclaiming a message that society doesn't always want to hear…that we need to save and respect our God-given planet. Peter calls us to think differently and creatively…calling us to leave our comfort zones and act in 'future-thinking' modes now."

Peter Wege began supporting the Boy Scouts as a young father when his sons got into Scouting. In 1966, Wege was elected vice-president of the Grand Valley Boy Scouts of America. Fair minded as always, four decades later Wege made sure he evened it up when the Girl Scouts needed help.

In 2003, the Girl Scouts of Michigan Trails wanted to upgrade and expand their Anna Behrens Camp in Greenville. With environmental education a big part of their Scouting program, the Girl Scout leaders were eager to honor Wege's LEED requirement for green building. Wege signed on for a $50,000 gift to the camp's capital campaign, including a new dining room.

In a letter thanking him for encouraging LEED building, the Girl Scout's executive director Lorena Palm told Wege they had run into an unexpected environmental hurdle. Fifty-one mature red pines grew on the only piece of land that could accommodate the new dining room. Rather than chop them down, the Michigan Trails Girl Scouts had an idea.

They'd found a local logging company that could prepare the pines to be used as columns, joists, and rafters in the high-ceilinged dining room. Instead of ending up as firewood, the stately red pines would be given a renewed life as the elegant focus of the room. Moreover, the Girl Scouts who helped design the new dining hall themselves had referred to it from the beginning as a "tree house."

In her letter to The Wege Foundation, Lorena Palm wrote, "Bringing the trees from the property inside will give a feeling of woods into the interior and teach an environmental lesson to our young women." And the final bonus was that reusing the red pines could add valuable LEED points.

Peter Wege didn't hesitate. He added another $200,000 to his gift for Camp Anna Behrens and the Girl Scouts, ensuring the girls would have their tree-house dining room. He also promised that their tree house would have solar energy so the sun could help keep it cool in the summer and warm in the winter.

At the same time Wege was helping the Girl Scouts, he was also into a project reflecting how so many of his donations had come to pass. They start with a friendship. This friend was Peter's archivist Diane Johnson who commuted to her job from Chase in Lake County.

Chase Township Public Library

Since books are life's blood to archivists, when Diane and her husband moved to Chase, she went looking for the library in her new town of 1,000 people. She found it housed in one-third of a dilapidated old schoolhouse, the rest of the 70-year-old building unheated and falling down.

Built in 1935 during the New Deal as a WPA project, the library had been a K-8 school until 1969. When Diane asked if there were any plans to fix it up, with Lake County the poorest in Michigan, the librarian could only shrug her shoulders and answer, "No money."

The next week while working in the Foundation offices in Peter's home, Diane casually mentioned the run-down library and its potential for the low-income area. Diane immediately found out what so many of Peter's friends had experienced. That was all he needed to hear. "Let's do something about it," was his simple response.

But if the Chase Library restoration grew out of Wege's friendship for Diane Johnson, it also matched three major Wege Foundation missions: education, environment, and serving the underserved. The people of Chase were paying attention. So grateful was the community, they leveraged Peter's $95,000 gift into far more by providing most of the sweat labor themselves.

Over three and a half years, these appreciative Lake County folks stripped the building to the studs so the plumbing and electricity could be updated. With the drywall finished, the volunteers rolled up their sleeves and stained and painted the walls. The Wege Foundation had the original wood floors sanded and stained, the parking area paved, and donated Steelcase furniture to complete the transformation.

By the time The Wege Foundation staff made a tour in the fall of 2004, the Chase Township Public Library was already the heart of the community. An article in The *Cadillac News* in March, 2006, was headlined: "Library brings the world to Chase." The article credits The Wege Foundation for "a morphing of the library into an open community hub."

The expanded and renewed space is where the young children of working parents come after school to find warmth and stories and companionship. They read, play games, do puzzles, and use the six computer stations. High school kids come to do homework and Internet research. And adults and senior citizens find their way to the library for books—but also for fellowship and friendship.

The Historical Society holds monthly meetings for history buffs. Their chief pride is a 6-foot Civil War Veteran's Post flag hanging behind the checkout desk. The library also displays art works on a rotating basis that include, not surprisingly, some of Peter Wege's personal collection. The changing art display offers Lake County the exposure to the arts they wouldn't otherwise have in their rural community.

The outdoor environment is almost as important and the library patrons take great pride in their Reading Garden. In 2003, volunteers converged with shovels and donated plants to create a 3,700 square-foot garden lush with variety and benches where readers could enjoy a book in the company of trees and flowers. Volunteers make sure that every spring 600 tulips announce the opening of the Reading Garden.

Thanks to Diane's offhand comment and Peter Wege's instinctive generosity, this once run-down building now hosts preschool story hour, summer reading programs, adult book discussions, Monopoly and Scrabble tournaments, arts and crafts, copy machines and faxes, plus a meeting room for the residents of Lake County.

Thanks to Peter always wanting to support his friends, the families of Lake County have a clean, well-lighted place where they can go to expand their horizons—educationally, environmentally, and socially.

As Diane Johnson puts it, "Thanks to 'himself,'" referring to Peter Wege, "Chase Library is now the centerpiece of the community and draws people from other townships and counties."

Signs posted at Blandford Middle School's garden

CHAPTER TWENTY EIGHT

BLEKE, BLANDFORD, AND THE STUDENT ADVANCEMENT FOUNDATION

"WHAT IS INEXCUSABLE ABOVE ALL ELSE IS OUR WORLD'S UNCONTROLLED POPULATION GROWTH...TOO MANY PEOPLE FOR TOO FEW RESOURCES WILL BRING CATASTROPHIC DESTRUCTION TO THE ECO-SYSTEM."

PETER M. WEGE,
ECONOMICOLOGY: THE ELEVENTH COMMANDMENT.

If Peter Wege's best known epitaph is "environmental visionary," his reputation could as easily center on his commitment to education. For Peter, the children of low-income families learning to read in the cozy Chase Library perfectly fit his mission.

Bert Bleke, a long-time school administrator, knew about Wege's passion for educating underprivileged children. So in 2002 when Bleke gave up his secure superintendent's job in Lowell to take on the challenge of leading the troubled Grand Rapids Public Schools, Bert knew where to go for help. He'd learned some important things about Peter Wege when they'd worked together creating the Wittenbach-Wege Enviromental Center in Lowell.

Bleke knew, that unlike many suburban residents, Peter Wege understood that the city's schools are everybody's schools—and everybody's responsibility. Bleke also knew Wege and he shared one mind-set: the children of the inner city have the same right to the best possible public education as do the children living in the wealthier surrounding suburbs.

Working toward educational equity, Bleke the educator and Wege the executive partnered up in 2003 to hire the best team they could find. Called the Harvard Leadership Change Group, the Ivy League educators signed a three-year contract and went to work. By the end of the contract, Bleke reported that the Harvard educaters had "essentially created an organization that is 180 degrees different in how we approach our work."

They made the GRPS administrators and teachers ask themselves, "Why are we here and for whom?" "How do we define 'excellence' in education?" Once defined, "How do we implement it so everyone knows what is expected and how to achieve it?"

The GRPS's out-dated randomness, according to Bleke, was replaced by a constructive pressure to perform up to certain, clearly defined standards. By 2006, school leaders from surrounding communities, including Rockford and Byron Center, were working with GRPS to implement Harvard Leadership Change in their own school systems.

Looking back on the impact this Harvard Leadership change has made, in 2017 GRPS Superintendent Teresa Weatherall Neal wrote this:

" In 2013, Peter Wege had the foresight to financially support Grand Rapids Public Schools to learn alongside Harvard Graduate School of Education's Change Leadership Group of improvement grant from the Steelcase Foundation, GRPS continues to learn

Peter Melvin Wege 1920-2014

Blandford School's working greenhouse.

The chicken sculpture on Blandford School's grounds honors the chicken each student raises every year. It also explains why they call themselves BEEPs, the acronym for Blandford Environmental Education Program.

with Harvard's professional education programs building transformational leadership deep in the system.

"In the past five years, the district has increased graduation rates, attendance, student achievement and enrollment. GRPS is moving in the right direction. I want to thank Mr. Wege and the Steelcase Foundation for the on-going support and belief in GRPS."

Making the Harvard rethink happen in GRPS was only part of Wege's legacy to the city schools. When Blandford Nature Center and Blandford School, a wildlife nature center and school in northwest Grand Rapids, lost its funding from the Public Museum, the museum board handed it off to the cash-poor GRPS.

With no money to save the nature center created in the late 1960s, Superintendent Bleke knew closing it would be a huge loss to kids and the community. He also knew of only one person who would consider saving it.

The staff and volunteers at Blandford Nature Center are quick to say that the doors would have closed in 2006 without Peter Wege. No longer could the thousands of visitors come through every year to learn about wildlife, tap maple trees for syrup, learn zoology, study botany, and walk the nature trails.

As Bleke put it, "In my mind, no Peter Wege—no Blandford Nature Center." But because Wege refused to let the Nature Center close, every year all the third-, sixth-, and ninth-grade students in the GRPS get to spend a school day at Blandford. "Many of these urban children," Bleke says, "never have the opportunity to be in nature."

In 2009, the 143-acre Blandford Nature Center left Kent County to become a 501 C-3 non-profit funded by private donations. The first giver to step up when the taxpayers could no longer keep it going was, of course, The Wege Foundation. Peter Wege made a five-year commitment to fund Blandford from 2009 until 2014.

That year Annoesjka Steinman became Blandford's first executive director. Steinman's background perfectly fit the newly evolved Blandford as a premier nature center that would need to be paid for by community donations. With a background in

Mary Jane Dockery, founder of the Blandford Nature Center and Blandford School.

environmental science and a history working for the Community Foundation for Muskegon County, Steinman understood both the natural science of Blandford Nature Center and the need to raise money for its ongoing support.

With Blandford Nature Center secured by private funding, it was time to address Blandford School's aging portable classrooms. In February 2013, a new 7,000 square-feet LEED construction opened its doors as Blandford School's first permanent building, the result of an unprecedented GRPS public-privae partnership.

Sixty sixth-graders left their rusted, leaky classrooms to enter twice the space in a new high-tech school. Not only did the new Blandford School feature the latest environmental advancements in construction, it also established an historic financing standard.

With the lead $1.5 million gift from The Wege Foundation—plus other private donors—added to the GRPS's funds, the $2.3 million school served as a template for more private-public funding in education. One highlight in the new school is the mosaic created by the 2012 BEEPs—Blandford Environmental Education Program students—honoring the school's founder, Mary Jane Dockery.

The colorful mosaic features a woman kneeling in a garden showing some delight of nature to a young student. Flowers, birds, even some salamanders faithfully depict the legendary Mary Jane's devotion to nature in all its forms and beauty.

Once the Elks Country Club and then the Highlands, the former golf course is now permanently conserved as public green space inside the city of Grand Rapids. This photo taken from the old 18th green looks down what was once the tenth hole, an overgrown cart path visible on the right.

In early 2017, an historic real-estate deal doubled the Nature Center's property next door to Blandford School. That year the Land Conservancy of West Michigan took over the 121-acre former Highlands Golf Course adjacent to the Center. The Wege Foundation, the Grand Rapids Community Foundation, the Ken and Judy Betz family, and the Cook Foundation made the lead gifts to buy the property.

Adding the former golf course's 121 acres to Blandford's 143 acres means the Nature Center now has 264 acres of permanently preserved green space open to the public inside the city limits of Grand Rapids.

Instead of the proposed development of the Highlands into homes and condos, the century-old originally-Elks golf course is being converted back to its natural state that includes thriving wetlands and natural wildlife habitats.

For The Wege Foundation, this property has special meaning because it's contiguous to Saint Anthony of Padua Catholic School headed by Father Mark Przybysz, the late Peter Wege's priest and close friend. Peter Wege had taken pride in building Father Mark's rectory as a pioneering green home and adding classrooms for the school. Now several of Peter's favorite causes—St. Anthony's School and Villa Verde and Blandford Nature Center and Blandford School—are next-door neighbors.

In 2017 Blandford's new visitor's center opened, again with support from The Wege Foundation, as the Mary Jane Dockeray Visitor Center. But the Blandford board hadn't forgotten who'd saved them a decade earlier. The original Blandford Nature Center's visitor's building is now the Peter M. Wege Environmental Education Center.

Peter Melvin Wege 1920-2014

Blandford Nature Center's new visitors center has been named for its founder, the Mary Jane Dockery Visitors Center.

Four Blandford BEEPs holding their own chickens and one BEEP getting to know a pond friend.

Blandford recognized Peter when he could no longer refuse the naming honor. By putting his two favorite causes in the name, they gave their late friend a most fitting tribute.

Former GRPS Superintendent Bert Bleke later said of Peter Wege, that besides saving Nature Center and spearheading a new Blandford School building, one of Wege's most important contributions was supporting the creation of the Student Advancement Foundation for the Grand Rapids Public Schools starting in 1993.

As with any cause that helped the K-12 students in his hometown's public schools, Peter Wege didn't hesitate to join nine other major donors to become, as the Student Advancement Foundation stationery reads, a *Founding Scholar* with a $30,000 gift.

The moving force behind the Student Advancement Foundation was GRPS's financial crunch in the early 1990s that forced high schools to charge students to play sports. The school system's pay-to-play program meant a lot of student-athletes couldn't be on a team because their families couldn't afford the uniforms.

The new Student Advancement Foundation came to be when the founders recognized the importance of sports in the lives of the city's young people. The SAF's earliest grants paid for uniforms so that all GRPS students could play sports. And those initial donations set the stage for what would become a multi-million dollar support system for Grand Rapids Public School students in all aspects of K-12 educaton.

That leap from small and sports to becoming an all encompassing school foundation started in 2003. That year GRPS's new superintendent Bert Bleke told Joan Secchia and her fellow SAF board members that the sleepy SAF needed to reinvent itself as a vibrant, healthy resource for the city's public schools. "Every urban school district needs a foundation," Bleke told the SAF board, "and you are ours."

As its first project, the newly regenerated SAF stocked all the GRPS schools' 40-plus libraries. True to his mantra to "Educate! Educate! Educate!" Peter Wege eagerly supported this first big initiative that put more than 400,000 new books in the GRPS schools' libraries.

The Wege Foundation continued making generous donations to the SAF as it grew into a vital resource for all GRPS students. By 2015, the SAF had given away $20 million in grants for K-12 education in the arts, environment, literacy, math, science, and physical wellness.

Peter Wege's generosity to Grand Rapids' Catholic schools was well known. With this in mind, Bert Bleke might have hesitated to approach Wege on behalf of the city's public schools. But he did because Bleke knew the man's heart—knew his love for children—and knew his passion for education.

Blandford Nature Center's original visitors building is now named for one of Blandford's greatest benefactors.

CHAPTER TWENTY NINE

GRAND RAPIDS POLICE, FIREFIGHTERS, AND WMCAT

"IT'S TIME FOR US ALL TO FIGHT TO SAVE THE EARTH. TODAY, NOT TOMORROW. I, FOR ONE, BELIEVE AMERICANS DO HAVE THE WILL TO KEEP THE PRESERVATION OF EARTH MOVING FORWARD IN HIGH GEAR."

ECONOMICOLOGY: THE ELEVENTH COMMANDMENT,
PETER M. WEGE.

While Peter Wege was proving himself a good friend to public education in Grand Rapids, he did not overlook the city's police department. As a show of his great respect for the law-enforcement profession, Wege generously supported the GRPD's Silent Observer that helps solve crimes through an anonymous tip line.

In fact, Wege's loyalty to Silent Observer was acknowledged in 1998 with the questionable "honor" of being roasted at their annual fund-raising dinner. Wege's fans and friends donned costumes to spoof their hero, with one skit on his endless support for Aquinas College. Dramatizing an Aquinas Board meeting, including a nun in habit, the cast depicted Peter listening to a long list of the college's budget needs.

"I'll do that," he'd interrupt. Or, "I'll take care of that." Or, "Just send me the bill." According to Sister Aquinas Weber, Peter's dear friend, one of the actresses and an Aquinas Board member, the skit wasn't far from what he really did at their meetings!

Making sure Silent Observer had enough funds was only one of Wege's acts of generosity to the Grand Rapids Police Department. When Harry Dolan came to Grand Rapids as the new Chief of Police in 1998, it didn't take long to discover Peter Wege's admiration for the dangerous work police officers do every day.

So when Chief Dolan wanted to honor the Grand Rapids police officers killed in the line of duty with a permanent memorial, he called on Peter Wege. Dolan later said Peter was "genuinely moved" by the idea of memorializing their fallen heroes. "Just get it done," Wege told the Chief. While many others contributed, Dolan said, "Peter Wege made it happen."

Dolan called Peter Wege "a kind-hearted man" who became his friend. Their relationship triggered another gift that made a little police history. On Monday, September 12, 2005, GRPD cruisers shut down Monroe Street not for a criminal pursuit, but for an historic announcement. The police department was about to get the first hybrid police car in the state and maybe in the country.

Who else but economicologist Peter Wege would give the GRPD his own new hybrid Ford Escape SUV freshly repainted police blue! The license plate significantly read: GR1HYBR. In addition to the red-and-white police lettering on the doors, the back panel featured the city's familiar Calder logo and the telltale word, "GREEN." Wege was particularly gratified when he found out his hybrid would be used by officers enforcing code violations since those infractions were often environmentally destructive.

Members of the Grand Rapids Police Department, including the bomb-sniffing dog aptly named Kilo. Peter M. Wege was an admirer and long-time supporter of both his hometown's police and fire departments.

Ever the educator, Wege also saw the hybrid police car as a teaching tool. The high visibility of this "green" police car driving around Grand Rapids would raise awareness of environmentally friendly cars. In accepting the gift, Chief Dolan noted the GRPD "wants to be innovative and Peter is showing us how…he's always been ahead of the curve on the environment."

Peter also supported the GRPD's Camp O'Malley, a summer camp in Caledonia started in 1942 by Police Chief Frank O'Malley to give vulnerable young people an outdoors experience with the police force serving as mentors. In 2012 the 600 at-risk children at Camp Malley got to interact with live birds and animals brought in by Holland's Outdoor Discovery Center thanks to Peter and The Wege Foundation. The Discovery staff also takes campers kayaking on the adjoining Thornapple River where they experience nature in ways many never have before.

Neither did Peter Wege neglect the city's other Public Safety branch, the Grand Rapids Fire Department, as he made two major gifts. One was a six-wheel amphibious, all-terrain rescue vehicle. The second was a command-post radio system to enhance fire-police communications in a major community disaster.

"We have to work together on these things," Peter Wege said about fire-police interaction. "These donations give me a chance to help our city's outstanding police and fire departments collaborate for everybody's benefit."

In 2003 Peter Wege got involved with all Kent County's police departments on a potentially explosive racial issue. Peter Wege was always on the side of the angels when anything hinted of racism. At the time, the African American community was accusing area police departments of "racial profiling" for pulling over a disproportionate number of minority drivers.

Grand Rapids high school students are shown at the West Michigan Center for Arts and Technology participating in their arts projects. In 2008, the 200-plus WMCAT students—who come after school to supplement their arts and technology educations moved into a 22,000-square-foot area on the top floor of a new four-story building on the West Side allowing more GRPS teenagers to join WMCAT. The expanded new space was the result of a $7.5M capital campaign supported by The Wege Foundation.

When the Kent County Chiefs of Police, the ACLU, and the Racial Justice Institute met to address the issue, they included one of the area's best known humanitarians for financial support. After extensive discussions, they concluded that both the police and the drivers needed to be educated on proper behavior in a traffic stop.

The result was a glove-compartment envelope designed to hold car registrations and insurance documents if a driver is pulled over. One side of the envelope lists the rules drivers need to follow —stay in the car with both hands in sight. The other side listed the police officer's rules—being "polite, courteous, respectful, and professional." With Wege's support, this widely distributed envelope aimed at defusing a racially sensitive issue.

Around the time area racial profiling was being addressed, several Steelcase leaders, including Jim Welch, Steelcase president Jim Hackett, and Peter M. Wege, along with GRPS Superintendent Patricia Newby flew to Pittsburgh to meet Bill Strickland. A gang member growing up, Strickland had been headed in the wrong direction until he stumbled on pottery making.

Because this creative activity saved him from street life, he'd devoted himself to doing the same for other teenagers by creating after-school educational opportunities for them. Called Make the Impossible Possible, Strickland's program offered art classes as a constructive way to explore new avenues of creative learning and career training.

Steelcase executive and grandson of founder Henry Idema, Jim Welch was the spark plug behind the trip to Pittsburgh. Newly retired, Welch's experience with Abundant Life Ministries encouraged him to replicate Strickland's model in Grand Rapids. Thus in 2005 the West Michigan Center for Arts and Technology opened in the old Jacobson's Store downtown.

WMCAT gives GRPS high school students a friendly place to go after school where they can learn photography, fine arts, graphic design, fiber arts, and digital art in a high-tech space. Adults are also offered classes in medical billing that can lead to good jobs.

Peter Wege's heart for kids, education, and the underserved guaranteed he'd be a WMCAT supporter. In the first two years he gave $200,000 as personal gifts and another $250,000 from The Wege Foundation. By 2015, between Peter's private donations and The Foundation's, WMCAT had received $680,000. With the support from Wege, Jim Welch, and Steelcase president Jim Hacket, it was only natural that WMCAT would be outfitted with furniture donations carrying the Steelcase label.

The cover of the booklet launching the national campaign to preserve and protect the Great Lakes.

CHAPTER THIRTY

PETER WEGE'S 'MOST IMPORTANT PROJECT'

> "I DO NOT FEEL OBLIGED TO BELIEVE THAT THE SAME GOD WHO HAS ENDOWED US WITH SENSE, REASON, AND INTELLECT HAS INTENDED US TO FOREGO THEIR USE."
>
> GALILEO GALILEI.
> *ECONOMICOLOGY II,*
> PETER M. WEGE.

If all his extensive philanthropy since 1967 hadn't accomplished enough, Peter had another "impossible" dream. Except for him, there was no such adjective. And so one day in early 2004 he announced to his staff, "We need to save the Great Lakes." And by May, he started to make it happen.

Saving the five Lakes began during a three-day meeting at Steelcase called Healing Our Waters sponsored by The Wege Foundation, along with the Frey, Beldon, and Charles Stewart Mott Foundations. Over 70 national experts in environmental policy, science, and economics had accepted Peter Wege's invitation to participate in this working conference.

Among them were leaders from the National Parks and Conservation Association; The Wilderness Society; the National Wildlife Federation; the Union of Concerned Scientists; U.S. Public Interest Research Group, and the Natural Resources Defense Council. Former president of the National Wildlife Federation Mark Van Putten, now CEO of The Wege Foundation, was a key organizer. Van Putten spoke to the power of these assembled leaders in saying they represented "millions of Americans."

In his letter inviting these national leaders to Grand Rapids, Peter Wege had written, "Our objective is to collaboratively reach consensus on a policy statement for restoring the Great Lakes ecosystem. We will focus not on the problems, but the solutions." He asked the attending experts to "develop a powerful statement on the policy reforms needed to begin the healing." He called that "powerful statement" the Magna Carta of the Great Lakes.

This 2004 Great Lakes conference was not just one more good cause for Peter Wege. Rather he described it as "the most important single project of my life as an environmental activist since starting The Wege Foundation in 1967."

Those three dynamic days in May 2004 were packed with long work sessions and lively debate as the environmental experts finally narrowed down the three biggest threats to the Great Lakes: invasive species, toxic pollution, and threatened water quality. They unanimously agreed keeping out exotic species had to be a top priority. These scientists knew that once foreign aquatic species enter the Great Lakes, they can rarely be eradicated.

Peter Melvin Wege 1920-2014

Healing Our Waters
An Agenda for Great Lakes Restoration

...d my life as they have so... ...commitment to restoring... ...andchildren's future.

President Gerald R. Ford in a letter to Peter M. Wege
July 26, 2006

The conference launching the restoration of the Great Lakes was held at Steelcase in May 2004. This sculpture in the Steelcase lobby signifies the three days of work sessions over 70 environmental scientists spent that culminated in a specific plan to fight what they named as the Lakes' most serious threats.

The Healing Our Waters (HOW) participants concluded that the federal government had not implemented policies already on the books for cleaning up contaminated sediments in Great Lakes' harbors and riverbeds. The government had also failed to remove concentrated toxic pollution and was still not holding the polluters accountable for the contamination.

Wege's invited guests also outlined a program to deal with the problem of deteriorating water quality in the Great Lakes that contains 21 percent of the world's surface fresh water and 84 percent of North America's.

On September 29, 2004, Peter Wege, as a private citizen, flew his staff to Washington, D.C. where he hosted a Congressional reception in the U.S. Capital promoting the HOW conference's recommendations—Wege's 'Magna Carta.' West Michigan's U.S. Congressman Vernon Ehlers, the only nuclear physicist in Congress and a widely respected environmentalist, thanked Wege for his leadership and assured the crowd he would do everything he could to get the federal government's financial support.

Congressman Ehlers kept his word. Within months, Ehlers' name was listed as one of 42 co-sponsors in the House of Representatives and seven Senators on a $20 billion package of proposed laws called the Great Lakes Collaboration Implementation Act. Congressman Ehlers scheduled congressional hearings where the HOW Coalition presented its case for legislation to address the threats the HOW conference had outlined.

Tom Kiernan, President of the National Parks Conservation Association and a participant in the HOW conference at Steelcase, said of Peter Wege's efforts, "At this stage in his life, Peter Wege could be doing many other things. But instead he is in the trenches, creating and leading coalitions to restore the Great Lakes and the environment upon which all life depends."

Personally funded by Peter M. Wege, in 2008 the Great Lakes Coalition met in Washington, D.C. under the leadership of West Michigan's late U.S. Congressman Vern Ehlers.

With this Great Lakes initiative, Peter Wege's goal was to bring together the various environmentalist groups and philanthropists who had worked for years—but often independently—on protecting the Great Lakes. Wege's call for collaboration was answered in 2005 when some 50 national, regional, state, and environmental groups created the Healing Our Waters-Great Lakes (HOW-GL) Coalition.

Funded by a five-year, $5 million grant—one million from Peter personally, the rest from The Wege Foundation, the HOW-GL was patterned after the Everglades Coalition that had successfully won government funding to protect the Everglades.

On December 12, 2005, at a press conference on the Chicago shore of Lake Michigan, the president of the National Parks Conservation Association Tom Kiernan announced the new collaboration and its blueprint for restoring the Lakes. "This is the first time in history," Kiernan told the audience, "that we've had a single plan to restore and protect the Great Lakes. And this is the first time in history that federal, state, tribal, and municipal governments have joined with the citizens of the region to unite behind the same plan."

Co-chairing this newly formed HOW-GL coalition with Kiernan was Andy Buchsbaum, director of the National Wildlife Federation's Great Lakes office. Buchsbaum confirmed the dire findings that had come out of the HOW conference in Grand Rapids by saying, "The Great Lakes are sick." But Buchsbaum also reiterated the hopefulness the HOW participants had expressed about the restoration initiative. "If we quickly take the actions in this plan, we can heal the Lakes."

Thanks to Peter Wege's collaborative vision, some heavy hitters had signed on, including Ohio Governor Robert Taft, Chicago Mayor Richard Daley, Tribal Leader Frank Ettawageshik, and Congressmen Mark Kirk and Vernon Ehlers.

By late 2006, on the banks of the Grand River that flows into Lake Michigan, with TV cameras whirring, U.S. Representative Vern Ehlers, joined by other federal and state leaders, again championed the HOW program Peter Wege had initiated. "If we can make this the number one environmental problem in the country," Congressman Ehlers told the crowd, "we can get a lot of help."

As Larry Schweiger, President and CEO of the National Wildlife Federation, put it, the result of Wege's $5 million pledge to support the Coalition "has been swift and sweeping." The Coalition quickly grew to 85 organizations from schools to businesses to government.

Over eight months of meetings in 2005, the HOW-GL Coalition brought over 1,500 GL citizens together to draft the first comprehensive Great Lakes Restoration Strategy. Chicago Mayor Richard M. Daley wrote about what had been accomplished. "With enthusiasm, devotion, and an impressive investment of time and financial resources, Mr. Wege brought government, non-profit, and private stakeholders together to address water quality and conservation issues."

In the spring of 2007, two Democrats and two Republicans from Great Lakes states—Senators Levin and Voinovich and Representatives Ehlers and Emanuel—introduced the Great Lakes Collaboration Implementation Act of 2007. With the Lakes holding over one-fifth of the world's fresh surface water, preserving them was a cause that transcended party lines.

The HOW-GL Coalition launched a national citizens campaign to bombard elected officials with letters of support. In the summer of 2007, Peter personally funded a national postcard mailing featuring Ed Gargin's Great Lakes photos that urged Americans to ask their Congressmen to support the Great Lakes legislation.

As Larry Schweiger, President and CEO of the National Wildlife Federation put it, "Peter's vision, passion, pragmatism, and financial support have made all of this possible. In just two years, he has changed the future course of the Great Lakes…Peter's leadership has been responsible for sparking a huge citizen uprising for the Great Lakes."

The How Coalition took a major leap forward in June 2008, just four years after The Wege Foundation's Steelcase conference, with an international agreement that prohibits taking water out of the Lakes.

Besides naming the three major threats to the Great Lakes, HOW's mission was also to make sure drier parts of the United States could not draw on the Great Lakes' water. In 2008 the Great Lakes Water Resources Compact took effect when it was signed by two Canadian provinces in the basin, Ontario and Quebec, along with Michigan, Minnesota, Indiana, Illinois, New York, Wisconsin, Ohio, and Pennsylvania. The Compact prohibits new or increased diversions of water outside the Great Lakes basin.

A quote on glass at the Lacks Cancer Center by Mahatma Gandhi could easily have been written about Peter Wege when he took on saving the Great Lakes. "We must become the change we want to see."

CHAPTER THIRTY ONE

KENNEDY'S HERO AND MELANIE'S SPARROWS

"Peter – YOU are my hero! Thanks for your leadership in the biggest fight to save the planet."
Robert F. Kennedy

Peter Wege had used his faith in the power of grassroots "citizen uprisings" to get national support for saving the Great Lakes. When Robert F. Kennedy, nephew of the late President John F. Kennedy, returned to Grand Rapids in 2005, he confirmed Peter's belief.

In 2001 delivering the Aquinas Wege Lecture, Kennedy had talked about the citizens' outrage over corporate polluting of New York's rivers that led to the Riverkeeper volunteers patrolling for any dumped pollutants. In 2005, Kennedy was back in Grand Rapids speaking to a full house at Steelcase during a two-day conference titled "Green By Design" on the best environmental building practices.

Robert F. Kennedy was asked to talk about his book *Crimes Against Nature*–the 'crimes' of increased pollution and strip mining caused by rollbacks in the Clean Air and Clean Water Act.

During his lecture, Robert Kennedy vigorously praised both Peter Wege and Steelcase. Kennedy said that in speeches he gives around the country, when he gets demonized as an anti-business tree hugger, he counters by naming three financially successful major corporations highly respected as environmental stewards. Steelcase is one of them. Patagonia clothing and Interface carpeting are the other two.

"Peter Wege is a mainstream corporate leader," said Kennedy. Paraphrasing Wege's term "economicology," he added, "Good environmental policy is identical to good economic policy… We damage our economy when we damage our finite natural resources. Environmental injury is deficit spending."

When he signed a copy of his book *Crimes Against Nature* for Peter, Kennedy wrote, "Peter – YOU are my hero! Thanks for your leadership in the biggest fight to save the planet."

In calling Peter Wege his environmental "hero," Robert F. Kennedy was unknowingly carrying on a tradition. Peter Wege had been almost the same age as Kennedy when he named Health Education and Welfare Secretary John Gardner his environmental hero. Gardner's *A Strategy For A Livable Environment* turned the Steelcase executive and heir into a passionate environmentalist.

The opening sentence of Gardner's Summary Statement could have been said by both Peter Wege and Robert F. Kennedy when he wrote, "America's affluence today contaminates the nation's air, water, and land faster than nature and man's present efforts can cleanse them."

In the early years of the 21st Century, Peter Wege got involved in two new projects that between them honored all The Wege Foundation's missions. One was the Baxter Community Center, an inner-city non-profit that grew out of the Grand Rapids race riots in late July 1967.

That's when members of the Eastern Avenue Christian Reformed Church decided to heal the divisions in their own racially mixed neighborhood. In 1967 the church converted the former Baxter Christian School into a haven for their neighbors white and black to gather as a community in a safe and supportive setting.

Baxter began offering recreation and tutoring, but before long the founders saw the families coming there needed more. That's when Baxter Community Center began adding preschool classes, day care, adult literacy, and counseling. The Center's founding message was "to reveal God's love by Christian witnessing to the spiritual, physical, emotional, social, and academic growth of the less fortunate, not only in words, but in deeds."

For over half a century, this faith-based program has welcomed people of every faith, color, and age with the same caring arms and has continued adding services that meet their families' "human needs" in practical ways.

A medical clinic. A dental clinic. Child care. Mental-health counseling. A marketplace with free clothing, food, and household goods. Tax preparation. Budget counseling. Tutoring. Mentoring. Long-time Executive Director Melanie Beelen is proud of the fact that each new program came from the Baxter clients themselves. "If only we could have a…" was the way a new service started.

By the start of the 21st Century when it was clear that meeting all these human needs required more room than the old Baxter Christian School had, they turned to the community for help. Baxter launched a $2.4 million Opening Doors capital campaign to remodel and expand their space.

Peter Wege's name came up early as he was already beloved at Baxter for restoring their neighborhood's business district on Wealthy Street. They knew about his loyalty to his home town—how he'd helped rejuvenate the area around his own first home on South Division. They knew he cared deeply about underprivileged children and their families.

And, once again, friendship played a role. Peter's good friend and Steelcase associate Dick Becker was on the Opening Doors campaign cabinet. Dick invited Peter and Ellen Satterlee to visit Baxter Center and see the good work going on there every day. Dick Becker was not surprised when Peter was quickly won over.

However, at the very time the Baxter leaders approached The Wege Foundation, Peter was adding his history-making requirement that he wouldn't support any new construction unless it was LEED certified. So on the spot, in typical Peter form, Wege made Baxter Center's Executive Director Melanie Beelen an offer. He would donate $250,000 for the construction if it was done according to the United States Green Building Council's LEED program.

Grateful as Melanie and the board members were for Wege's offer, they knew the higher cost for building green wasn't in their budget. But they were also resourceful. Using Wege's offer with Baxter's donor base for leverage, the Center applied for a Kresge Challenge grant of $175,000. With the credibility of The Wege Foundation in place, Kresge came back with a firm, "Yes."

It turned out Wege's insistence on LEED building became a huge asset to the fundraising when Melanie found out the Kresge Foundation also promotes green building. In order to encourage environmental construction, the Kresge Foundation gave out unrestricted "bonus grants" for non-profits if they built green. Baxter thus won a second grant from the Kresge Foundation for $150,000 in 2007 when the new addition passed the U.S. Green Building Council's inspection.

In gratitude for Wege's support, in 2004 Baxter presented Peter Wege with the St. Francis Award. Seven years later, in 2011, The Wege Foundation's CEO Ellen Satterlee would also be named a recipient of this honor given to people who model the Prayer of St. Francis of Assisi, "Lord, make me an instrument of your peace, and where there is hatred, let me sow love."

In 2012 The Wege Foundation again supported the Baxter Community Center's youngest clients by funding a colorful new room for toddlers. As the 2011 St. Francis Award winner, Ellen Satterlee used her "naming" opportunity to honor Baxter's devoted director Melanie Beelen by christening the room "Ms. Melanie's Sparrows" from the Bible's, "His eye is on the sparrow" about God's love for little children.

Melanie Beelen summarized Peter's effect on Baxter, "The strongest gift Peter has brought us and taught us is that life comes full circle. It's our belief that not one detail in life's circumstances gets wasted. Peter is not wasting his later years but using them for the greater good."

By 2005, Baxter's green initiatives were already paying back even before Kresge's bonus grant was paid. When heat and electricity costs hit historic highs that winter, Baxter's energy-efficient addition helped contain their utility bills. Once again, economicology in action.

Riverkeepers founder Robert F. Kennedy and Peter M. Wege after Kennedy delivered the 2001 Aquinas Wege Lecture.

CHAPTER THIRTY TWO

FARMLAND PRESERVATION: WIN-WIN FOR ECONOMICOLOGY

"THIS FARM, WELL, IT'S LIFE TO ME."
LLOYD FLANAGAN

The second major gift in the first decade of the 21st Century that honored The Wege Foundation's mission began one chilly May morning in 2006. Peter Wege dedicated the Lloyd and Kathleen farm in eastern Kent County that day as permanently preserved farmland. Seeing farm preservation as a major weapon against urban sprawl, Wege enabled the Flanagan family to save forever their 145 acres as farmland.

Thanks to a Kent County program called Purchase of Development Rights (PDR) and Wege's generosity, the Flanagan's land will be passed on to their son Dave who farms it. In the future, the land can be sold or leased to another farmer, but it can never be used for anything but a farm or open space.

This PDR program offers federal and state funds to farmers who want to preserve their farms forever. The restricting challenge is that the government dollars must be matched by local money. For the Flanagan farm, the $290,000 grant from the United States Farm and Ranch Lands Protection Program would get paid only if the same amount was raised locally.

Since Kent County refused to allocate any tax dollars to save fams, those federal funds would have been sacrificed, and the Flanagan farm sold for development had Wege and The Wege Foundation not stepped in. Combining the federal grant with funds from The Wege Foundation, and $11,575 from the Grand Rapids Community Foundation, the PDR program paid the Flanagans $4,000 an acre.

That price was the difference between their land's value as a subdivision at $6,100 an acre for development and its value as a farm which was $2,100 an acre. And since a farmer's land is his pension, that $4,000 an acre became Lloyd and Kathleen Flanagan's retirement fund and the only way they could have saved their cherished 145 acres as farmland.

For Peter Wege, saving Kent County's farmland from disappearing perfectly fit his passion for economicology. Urban sprawl degrades the environment while buying the Flanagan's development rights enriches the local farm economy. In 2006, agriculture was Kent County's fifth biggest industry generating $150 million in sales a year.

Knowing developers saw corn fields as money-making subdivisions, Wege knew that once a working farm gets paved over, it is gone forever. He also knew that Kent County had lost 12 percent of its prime farmland to urban sprawl in just five years between 1997 and 2002.

With support from Peter and The Wege Foundation, the Flanagan's family farm in Grattan Township is permanently preserved as farmland through the Purchase of Development Rights program.

Wege also understood the economic advantage for taxpayers in preserving farmland like the Flanagan's. Had the 145 acres been sold for development, county taxpayers would have had to foot the bill for new roads, water, sewer, schools, and public safety. And the taxpayers' costs to operate that infrastructure would always increase and never go away. Buying the Flanagan's development rights, on the other hand, was a one-time expense and done with.

For Lloyd Flanagan, what Wege did went beyond the money for retirement and for medical expenses related to his kidney transplant. The farm had been his home since his parents bought it in 1947 when Lloyd was six. First his parents, then Lloyd and Kathleen, and now their son David farm the land.

Lloyd struggled to express his gratitude to Peter Wege. With his farm preserved, the land he grew up on remains in the family. "My eyesight's not good enough to drive," Lloyd told Peter, "but I can still walk out in the fields, back out in the woods…it's hard to explain how much I appreciate what Mr. Wege did. This farm, well, it's life to me."

Farmers like the Flanagans have a sacred connection to their land. That is why between 2002 and 2005, the first three years of the PDR program, 110 Kent County farmers applied to have their land permanently preserved. And over those years and into 2007, 701 acres of farmland were forever preserved in West Michigan.

After the Flanagan farm Peter Wege and The Wege Foundation preserved a 72-acre farm belonging to Clayton and Mary Lou Heffron. The USDA Farm Protection program put up $154,800 for the Heffron's PDR rights, with matching funds from The Wege Foundation and the Grand Rapids Community Foundation.

The Wege Foundation went on to help buy the development rights for Vern and Gay Nauta's 74.5-acre farm on Parnell and Three Mile in Vergennes Township. The fourth Kent County farm that would not have been saved without Peter and The Wege Foundation was Marsha Wilcox's 56 acres at Three Mile Road and Murray Lake Road in Vergennes Township.

Peter's leadership on farmland preservation did not go unnoticed. In 2007, United Growth for Kent County gave Peter M. Wege its Land Use Stewardship Award. They recognized Wege and The Wege Foundation for supporting farmland preservation, public transit, water quality, green-building initiatives, and conservation.

In making the presentation, Paul Haan, President of the non-profit United Growth for Kent County Board of Directors, said: "Mr. Wege is being honored today for his commitment to positive land use in Kent County and throughout the state. Mr. Wege's leadership has made Grand Rapids the most LEED-certified city in the country."

To recognize Peter M. Wege's Stewardship Award, United Growth has placed a brick in the Grand Ideas Garden of the MSU Extension Center with his name on it. The brick, according to Paul Haan, "will remind visitors of Mr. Wege's commitments to our community."

In the first month of 2007, Peter Wege worked once again with friends from the land-conservation world. Executives from the Land Conservancy of West Michigan and those from Kent County's PDR Program joined forces with Wege and The Wege Foundation to preserve agricultural and rural land personally owned by Wege in eastern Kent County.

Mr. Wege donated conservation easements on his nine properties in an area of Vergennes Township called the Parnell Avenue Corridor where preserving farmland is a priority. Wege's gift of 577 acres for conservation easements increased the land preserved in the Parnell Corridor to 1,044 acres. Kendra Wills, executive director of the PDR program for the county, called Wege's personal land donation "one of most significant gifts ever in West Michigan."

Conservation easements benefit the public by saving important farmland and natural resources such as wildlife habitat and groundwater; and the Land Conservancy of West Michigan is committed to ensuring the preservation restrictions will be honored in the future.

"Donating conservation easements to protect my rural property from ever being developed is the most natural thing in the world for me to do," Peter Wege explained simply.

In March 2008 Peter Wege once again supported saving green space inside the city when he joined a public-private partnership called "Green Grand Rapids." Recognizing the health of the inner city affects all of Greater Grand Rapids, The Wege Foundation endorsed the city's aim of adding more green spaces instead of more parking lots.

Other collaborating funding partners for the $583,000 Green Grand Rapids included the City Commission, the Downtown Development Authority, the Frey Foundation, the Dyer-Ives Foundation, and the Grand Rapids Community Foundation. Then when Mayor George Heartwell set up a Community Sustainability Partnership, The Wege Foundation donated $100,000 a year for three years.

And the summer Grand Rapids could not afford to maintain the city's public pools, The Wege Foundation helped pay the bill so the city's children had a place to swim.

CHAPTER THIRTY THREE

SUPPORTING TREATMENT FOR A BRAIN DISEASE

"The Wege Foundation grant made all the difference to Turning Point and those it serves."

Jamie Muller, Salvation Army

In the same way the inner-city mission of the Baxter Community Center appealed to Peter Wege, so did the work of the Salvation Army, another Christian organization dedicated to the underserved. One of Peter's first gifts to The Salvation Army was a typically spontaneous action of generosity in the late 1990s.

The Salvation Army's Adult Rehabilitation Center (ARC) for adults recovering from alcoholism/addiction was housed in the building on South Division where Peter Martin Wege had opened Metal Office Furniture. In 1953 when MOF/Steelcase moved into a new building, the company donated the old factory to the Salvation Army. That Salvation Army connection to his father gave Peter a special feeling for the ARC program restoring lives because it is housed in the old MOF plant.

When Peter and his staff toured the former MOF plant, Peter had fun pointing out to their Salvation Army hosts where his dad's office had been on the second floor. "Now that used to be…" and "Here's where…" The Salvation Army officers were delighted to hear how the space devoted to rehabilitating lives was once used to make office furniture.

Over lunch with the beneficiaries living in the recovery center, Peter overheard a conversation about phones cutting out at the ARC. An officer explained that the men answering the phone to schedule pickup donations often cut the callers off because the system was so outdated.

"Well you can't have that if you depend on those donations to pay your bills," Peter said shaking his head. He'd just learned that the money to support the ARC and the 70-100 men living there came entirely from sales in the Salvation Army store on the main floor.

"Ellen," he said to his right hand Ellen Satterlee, "make a note to call the phone company tomorrow. Tell them to come out here and install a new system."

This was the Salvation Army's first exposure to Peter Wege, their impromptu guardian angel. The Army's leaders now understood why Mr. Wege's name was inevitably linked to words like "generous" and "caring" and "unassuming."

In early 2003, the Salvation Army faced an unexpected crisis. Its widely respected drug-and-alcohol inpatient program Turning Point had to move out of their space in Metropolitan Hospital on Boston by August 1 because the hospital was moving south of town.

Fortuitously that same spring, Turning Point had been invited to join a new six-agency consortium in the former Ferguson Hospital on Sheldon Avenue. Not surprisingly, this collaboration was coordinated by Peter's friend, Dwelling Place's Denny Sturtevant. Part of the consortium's offer was an entire floor available for Turning Point.

Too timely to be true, yes. But there was a sticking point. In order to qualify for Joint Commission Accreditation, a vital status the Turning Point's substance-abuse program had held for years, the available space at Ferguson would need expensive renovations the Salvation Army couldn't afford. The men and women in desperate need of the Turning Point's intensive medical, emotional, and spiritual treatment were faced with having no place to go when they left Metropolitan Hospital.

Time was short and the Salvation Army's Turning Point needed a friend. They knew Peter had supported the ARC and they also knew his compassion for helping the sick. This time the people seeking help were suffering from the brain disease of alcoholism and addiction.

Peter and his staff met with Salvation Army officers and Turning Point employees to hear their story. As Jamie Muller, Divisional Development Director for the Army, put it, "Mr. Wege caught the vision of the Salvation Army for relocating its treatment program to a quality facility connected to an innovative downtown collaboration." Wege's respect for both Denny Sturtevant and the Salvation Army sealed the deal.

A grant of $75,000 saved Turning Point. Within six months, on August 6, 2003, their recovering patients moved into a brightly renovated floor at Ferguson. They could hardly believe their eyes.

As Jamie Muller put it, "The Wege Foundation's grant made all the difference to Turning Point and those it serves."

Wege's generosity in funding the move to Ferguson yielded an unexpected financial win for the Salvation Army's substance-abuse program. Within five months, Turning Point erased its deficit. But the big win was for the many men and women fighting the hard battle for sobriety. The Ferguson site offered them a safer and more effective place to find recovery and restore their lives.

Within three years of Turning Point's move, every other in-patient "sub-abuse" program in town had closed its doors. Had Peter and The Wege Foundation not recognized this vital health need, there would have been no medically accredited in-patient residence in Grand Rapids to help people caught in the nightmare disease of addiction.

Peter Wege and The Wege Foundation were all about renewing and restoring. With this donation, it was human lives they were restoring.

Even the smaller grants from Peter Wege dramatically changed lives. One, in particular, stands out because it involved former Steelcase employee Kenny Hoskins. The senior pastor at the Divine Grace Church since its 1999 founding, Pastor Hoskins knew about Peter Wege's years of support for inner-city families. Hoskins also knew Peter from their shared work on Faith in Motion that succeeded in passing millages to expand bus service.

But the two really got acquainted during a Martin Luther King celebration at the Amway Hotel when Pastor Hoskins sat next to Peter at dinner. Kenny Hoskins told Peter about the Interdenominational Ministerial Alliance, a social-justice group of some 40 African American churches. Naturally, Peter Wege wondered what he could do to help.

The Ministerial Alliance wanted to motivate young black men by bringing to Grand Rapids successful African American males to serve as role models. Peter jumped on this great idea. With

Wege's help, Dr. Ben Carson, the first African American ever elected chief of neurosurgery at Johns Hopkins, was the first to share his story in Grand Rapids.

Dr. Carson, named head of the Department of Housing and Urban Development in 2017, told his audience how he grew up in poverty raised by a single mother who didn't know how to read. If he could become a neurosurgeon from that background, so could they.

Grateful for Wege's help funding the Ministerial Alliance's speakers, Pastor Hoskins didn't plan to ask Peter for anything else. Then in 2006, his Divine Grace Church faced a financial crisis. Over its seven years, the church had met at the Holiday Inn, the Forest Hills Christian Community Church, and East Congregational Church before ending up in the basement of the vacated Martin Luther King Park Church.

Divine Grace Church offered to buy the empty church if the seller paid for the necessary repairs, including the roof, furnace, carpeting, and paint. Days before the closing, the seller told Pastor Hoskins he wouldn't pay for any repairs, and the church stood to lose its down payment and the church.

Terri McCarthy, Program Director for The Wege Foundation, knew Pastor Hoskins from working with him on the Mayor's Environmental Action Council. Kenny Hoskins told Terri about his church's emergency. As always with Peter, when any of his staff members brought him a need, he listened.

His staff was like family and he knew they had good judgment. If they said a cause was worthy, that was good enough for him. But since Peter already respected Pastor Hoskins, rescuing their church was not a hard sell. On October 26, 2005, Peter Wege and Terri McCarthy looked on with joy as the members of Divine Grace Church celebrated and praised God while they dedicated their remodeled and freshly painted church.

For the first time since their founding, Divine Grace members didn't have to rent anyone's basement. Thanks to Peter and The Wege Foundation, they had their own church.

From the beginning days of The Wege Foundation, Peter had said repeatedly it would take the best academic minds in the country to save the environment. In April 2006, Peter M. Wege saw for the eighth time how he'd translated that belief into action. In 1999 Peter Wege had invited top environmental leaders from major universities to gather at Aquinas for the first ECONOMICOLOGY meeting.

At that inaugural gathering, Peter told the distinguished scholars, "It will take education and leadership from colleges and universities to meet the environmental challenges we face and leave a healthy world for our children and grandchildren. Together we can do this."

That original 1999 ECONOMICOLOGY meeting at Aquinas was attended by twenty academicians. By 2006 over 70 university and environmental leaders came representing fourteen colleges, including the University of California Santa Barbara, the University of Wyoming, and Cape Eleuthera Island School/Institute in The Bahamas.

Welcoming the guests filling Aquinas's Wege ballroom, Peter Wege called them "the finest group of environmental scientists and thinkers and writers in the whole country."

One was Dr. Rick Clugston who talked about the Earth Charter that grew out of the historic 1992 Earth Summit in Rio de Janeiro. The Earth Charter identified the planet's two most critical issues as protecting the environment and addressing socio-economic development. That Charter, now the global "Environmental Bill of Rights" endorsed by over 2,000 organizations, defines sustainability as "meeting the needs of the present without compromising the ability of future generations to meet their own needs."

Chris Maxey spoke about his Cape Eleuthera Island School in The Bahamas founded in 1999 to teach sustainability to students from grade school to the PhD level. In 2000 Peter Wege funded the Island School's shift to renewable energy by providing wind and solar power.

He followed that with over $500,000 to build the Wege Center for Sustainable Fisheries constructed, of course, according to sustainable, green design. He then added $100,000 worth of Steelcase furniture to outfit the new Wege Center.

The school's 2006 spring newsletter *Island News* wrote, "The Wege Center for Sustainable Fisheries is the focal point of our new campus and the place where people gather to listen and become inspired about how we can impact the future…"

Chris Maxey said of the Bahamas' national movement toward sustainability, "Only through the generous support of The Wege Foundation and Peter Wege has the shift toward clean energy become a reality for the country of the Bahamas."

The various presentations at Aquinas 2006 ECONOMICOLOGY sparked energetic discussions and networking. The intellectual synergy of working together to create what no single college could do alone affirmed the truth of what Peter Wege repeatedly said. "We have to collaborate…the problems are too big."

CHAPTER THIRTY FOUR

KENT COUNTY'S HABITAT FOR HUMANITY MAKES HISTORY

"We must begin the process of creating a quality of life that can sustain all of Earth's inhabitants decently and equitably."

Peter M. Wege,
Economicology: The Eleventh Commandment.

Peter's support for the Island School in The Bahamas was an exception to The Wege Foundation's focus on education in West Michigan. Indeed, Peter Wege's generosity to the Grand Rapids Public Schools was a long-standing priority. And Wege was particularly drawn to one GRPS school: the C.A. Frost Environmental Science Academy.

This K-8 school opened in 1992 as a magnet school for environmental science and character education in northwest Grand Rapids next to Blandford Nature Center. The school's proximity to Blandford's woods and trails gives Frost an outdoors venue inside the city limits. Indeed Frost School's motto is "Where No Child Is Left Inside!"

The diverse students who attend Frost Academy, both from the neighborhood and throughout the city, know they're lucky to get in because of waiting lists. The environmental science curriculum crosses all academic disciplines from reading to math to the social studies and the arts—especially writing. The character piece of Frost focuses on a different value every month, such as responsibility and fairness.

In May 2007, students in C.A. Frost Environmental Science Academy thanked Peter Wege for his $35,000 donation for new library books in a very special way. The K-8th graders greeted him as they sat along the halls reading books, all gifts from him. They also gave him a wooden bench they had made and adorned with colorful paintings of the outdoors. Wege thrilled them when he said it was such a work of art, he was going to put it in the new Grand Rapids Art Museum when it opened. And he did!

But the ceremony's highlight was the interactive poem the students performed with principal Pamela Wells about children who were sad because they had so few books to read. "Then hark!" Principal Wells said to the students gathered around her, "In the distance was a man like no one in the land of C.A. Frost had ever seen."

"Who? Who?" the children responded in unison.
"Mr. Peter Wege was his name," their principal answered,
"and planting seeds of knowledge was his game."
"Ohhhh," the children chorused.
"It was books that he brought to our land so green," Pamela Wells continued, "His wheelbarrow more full than we'd ever seen! Mysteries, fables, poems took sprout, We were finally at the end of our great book drought!"

Peter Wege never had more fun at a thank-you than he did at the one from students at C.A. Frost.

Students in Grand Rapids Community College's M-TEC program learning how to build according to the United States Green Building Council's LEED standards—Leadership in Energy and Environmental Design.

On October 22, 2007, Peter Wege realized every little boy's dream: he became a Fire Chief! No matter that it was an honorary title bestowed by the Grand Rapids Fire Department. On the Fire Chief's white helmet the gold letters read, *Chief Peter M. Wege*. It was the first time in the history of the GRFD that an honorary Fire Chief had ever been named.

One of Peter's gifts to the GRFD was a mobile-command radio system needed in case of a major disaster. In June 2008, that emergency radio equipment helped prevent a major tragedy when a helicopter crash-landed on Butterworth Hospital's helipad shooting flames and spilling gasoline. At the first 911 call, the GRFD used the radio system Wege had donated to mobilize all the necessary emergency support needed to put out the fire, evacuate the hospital, and prepare for mass casualties.

Fotunately the helicopter pilots were rescued from where they were hanging off the roof to avoid the fire. Patients were safely evacuated and doctors were standing by. But because of the speedy response, the GRFD got the fire out before it could spread. The Fire Department hoped they'd never need the mobile-command radio system Peter had given them, but they were grateful they had it that June morning.

As he'd given his hybrid SUV to the Police Department, so now Peter also gave the GRFD his own three-wheeled all-terrain-vehicle, allowing firefighters to move quickly into areas without roads. And one of his most valuable gifts was joining other foundations and donors to buy ten life-saving thermal-imaging cameras. Like night-vision glasses, these state-of-the-art cameras let firefighters see inside burning buildings to check if anyone's still there.

The thermal-imaging cameras have also saved firefighters' lives by recording the temperatures if they're in an area about to erupt in flames. The heat camera alerts them to evacuate the building immediately.

Grand Rapids firefighters would never see Chief Peter Wege sliding down the fire pole, but they always knew their first honorary Chief held them in high respect.

In the spring of 2004, Sandy Weir from Kent County's Habitat for Humanity heard Christine Ervin, CEO of the U.S. Green Building Council, deliver the Wege Lecture at Aquinas. Ervin talked about the connection between good stewardship and building green. Ervin made the case for economicology by noting that LEED-certified buildings cost more to build, but save utility costs in the long run.

That set Sandy Weir's wheels spinning. Why can't Habitat for Humanity build LEED homes?

Sandy took her brainstorm to the Habitat board members who endorsed the concept, but worried about the extra building costs. They encouraged Sandy Weir to explore the possibility. The fact no other Habitat home in the country was green-built didn't deter Weir. No other community had a Peter Wege whose speaker had done just what Wege intended with his lectures. Christine Ervin had stimulated interest in sustainable construction.

Peter Wege, of course, was the first person Habitat approached to cover the extra costs of building to LEED standards. His "yes" was swift. In 2006 the U.S. Green Building Council awarded this country's first ever "LEED Certified Affordable Home" to a Habitat house in Grand Rapids.

Even more significant, thanks to a $600,000 grant from The Wege Foundation, Habitat for Humanity of Kent County made the commitment to build all future homes by LEED standards.

Word soon got around that Grand Rapids Habitat for Humanity was building affordable houses that were also LEED certified. Habitat's phone did not stop ringing and Kent County's Habitat became a local, regional, and national model of energy-efficient construction for low-cost housing.

And Habitat soon found a whole new cadre of skilled LEED workers. In 2001, the year after Ervin's lecture, The Wege Foundation funded a partnership with Grand Rapids Community College to create a technical training program called the Tassell Michigan Technical Education Center. The Tassell Center teaches CC students, along with tenth-twelth graders from the Grand Rapids Public Schools, how to do LEED construction in the real-life lab of building and rehabbing houses for Habitat of Humanity.

Within a few years, this M-TEC was offering the same education in LEED building to older adults who'd lost jobs in the collapse of Michigan's manufacturing base. George Waite, director of Tassell M-TEC said, "All of our graduates will now have credentials and experience to work on green projects."

In 2007, the second green Habitat home went up, built by thirty GRCC students in the M-Tech program. Educated by their LEED-qualified instructors in the latest green-building practices, these GRCC builders now use their environmental skills in the community. The long-term effect of this educational experience is exactly what Peter Wege worked toward his entire life.

Some of the many volunteers who renovate and build homes for Habitat for Humanity of Kent County. Since Peter M. Wege and the Wege Foundation got involved, all Habitat construction follows LEED protocols.

The financial results of these pilot Habitat homes confirmed Wege's faith in economicology. Treat your ecology well and you will also help your economics. While it cost approximately $8,000 more to build the first Habitat home by LEED rules, homeowners could expect to save $1,000 a year on electricity, heat, and water. After eight years, the initial cost was paid back in utility bills. And with a homeowner's 25-year mortgage, over that time the

savings is $25,000 they can invest in their family's future instead of paying it to the utility companies.

As Peter Wege put it, "The fact that Habitat has already discovered their green-built homes will save the new homeowners money in utility costs is a perfect demonstration of economicology…

"I am also gratified that the Habitat people turned the green building into an education opportunity for students at Community College. I congratulate everyone involved in this historic achievement."

Pam Doty-Nation, Executive Director of Habitat for Humanity of Kent County, summarized the trend among Habitats across the country to construct LEED homes. "This is the right way to build, and we have The Wege Foundation to thank for showing us the way and empowering our journey to sustainability."

In 2014 sixteen Habitat homes opened in Wealthy Heights. Once a neglected neighborhood, Wealthy Heights homes were now highly prized for one reason dating back to 1997. That was the year when the Wealthy Street business district was in free-fall, and Peter Wege led the campaign to restore the area's most prominent building, Wealthy Theatre. In a ripple affect, businesses and restaurants came back, and by 2014 residences in Wealthy Heights were choice places to live.

The lucky families who got these Wealthy Heights Habitat houses worked hard for them. Each family had to spend 300-500 hours on construction plus taking extensive classes in home maintenance and money management. Habitat's front-door keys aren't just handed out; they are earned.

Sandy Weir, former Director of Development for Habitat for Humanity of Kent County, wrote after Wege's first LEED gift to Habitat for Humanity:

"Peter Wege's support empowered Habitat to build the FIRST LEED certified affordable home in the nation in 2006…bringing energy efficient practices to those who need it…Mr. Wege demonstrated that care of the environment can be very good for people…Indeed, he has given Habitat a new way of seeing itself as an affordable home builder in an environmental context… that has begun to resonate throughout the 1,700 national Habitat Affiliates."

CHAPTER THIRTY FIVE

HONORING THREE DECADES OF GOOD WORKS AND THE MAN BEHIND THEM

> "YOU REPRESENT THE BEST IDEALS OF THE UNIVERSITY OF MICHIGAN, AND WE ARE PROUD TO WELCOME YOU BACK IN ORDER TO PRESENT YOU WITH THIS HONORARY DEGREE."
> PRESIDENT MARY SUE COLEMAN TO PETER M. WEGE.

In December 2007, the University of Michigan—where Peter Wege once set a javelin-throwing record—paid him its highest tribute. During winter commencement ceremonies, the University of Michigan conferred on Peter M. Wege an honorary degree as a Doctor of Laws.

University of Michigan President Mary Sue Coleman introduced Wege to the graduating seniors and guests in Chrysler Arena: "Peter Melvin Wege has dedicated his life to improving global ecology through relentless persuasion, prodding people and organizations into undertaking initiatives and achieving results that never would have occurred without his advocacy. He has devoted over half a century of his own energy and resources to the University of Michigan and the State of Michigan."

Dr. Coleman told the audience that Wege left the University in his sophomore year to join the U.S. Army Air Corps after the bombing of Pearl Harbor. "He not only defended our nation against enemy forces," Dr. Coleman said, "but also realized we needed to protect our country against the harsh consequences of our own pollution…Mr. Wege became an early activist regarding the ecology of Michigan."

In 1967, she said, he created The Wege Foundation to honor his parents, Sophia Louise and Peter Martin Wege, principal founder of Steelcase. In noting Wege's support for the University, Dr. Coleman spoke about his service as the first chairperson of the advisory board for the National Pollution Prevention Center, now the Center for Sustainable Systems.

Coleman described him as "a robust supporter of the University's School of Natural Resources and Environment." Among his gifts, she noted, is the Peter M. Wege Lecture started in 2001 focused on education and the environment that had become one of the campus's most popular lectures.

In addition to sponsoring the Wege Lecture, President Coleman acknowledged Peter Wege's support for the sustainable renovation of the century-old Dana Building housing the School of Natural Resources and Environment. In 2005, the Dana Building received a gold rating from the U.S. Green Building Council making it the greenest academic building in Michigan. President Coleman spoke about his two books on economicology calling it "a word he coined to promote a balance between a healthy ecology and a profitable economy." In presenting the Doctor of Laws diploma, Dr. Coleman concluded:

University of Michigan President Mary Sue Coleman presenting an honorary Doctor of Laws degree to Peter M. Wege during commencement ceremonies in December 2007.

"Mr. Wege, your extraordinary vision and deep-rooted commitment have made our planet a better place for future generations. You have shown us that it is not enough to be passionate about a cause, but that we need to translate our enthusiasm into action. By devoting your support to educational efforts as well as specific projects, you are ensuring that your mission will continue far into the future. You represent the best ideals of the University of Michigan, and we are proud to welcome you back in order to present you with the honorary degree."

The new Dr. Wege shared the stage with one of the world's scientific heavyweights, Francis S. Collins, M.D., Ph.D, who delivered the commencement address to the 2,000 Michigan seniors graduating that day. Dr. Collins headed the Human Genome Project that mapped and sequenced the human DNA starting in 1990 with the first draft published in 2000. Dr. Collins went on to become director of the National Human Genome Research Institute at the National Institutes of Health.

While the Univeristy of Michigan was honoring Peter Wege in 2007, so were a lot of little children in Grand Rapids, the result of a dream four women had ten years earlier. Georgia Woodrick Gietzen, Alyce Greeson, Carla Morris, and Aleicia Woodrick wanted to create a place where children could play in creative and hands-on ways.

They started with exhibits in a shopping center where over 30,000 children did play-work making things in a Funstruction and blowing bubbles in another space. This launch of what would become the Grand Rapids Children's Museum next moved into the public library and then to the Public Museum.

But the founders needed a permanent location, and they found it at 11 Sheldon Avenue downtown. That's when The Wege Foundation got involved. Knowing of Peter's generosity, his support for the City of Grand Rapids, and, above all, his love of children and education, the women knew it wouldn't be a hard sell.

It wasn't. In October 2007, Peter was honored by the Grand Rapids Children's Museum for being one of "The Ten Who Made A Difference" by helping it acquire its permanent two-story, play-learn facility on Sheldon and Fulton.

For a man who loved nothing better than a good belly laugh himself, supporting a place where children can learn *and* have fun was a no-brainer.

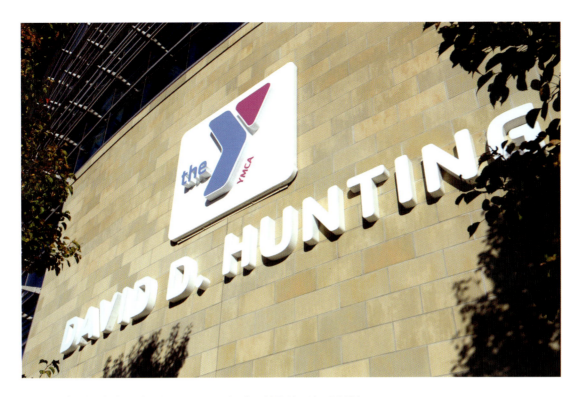

Named after his father's business partner the David D. Hunting YMCA.

Wege's honors from the University of Michigan and the Children's Museum came on the heels of Peter Wege's tribute from Michigan's Governor Jennifer Granholm. On May 20, 2006, at Detroit's Fox Theatre, Governor Granholm presented Peter Wege with the Russell G. Mawby Award for Philanthropy.

Named for the long-time head of the W.K. Kellogg Foundation, the Mawby Award goes to "an individual who has demonstrated a lifelong commitment to encourage private action for the public good." Movie star and Michigan resident Jeff Daniels was part of the Awards Ceremony that included a video highlighting some of Peter's good works in Grand Rapids.

Receiving the Russell G. Mawby Award had special significance for Peter as the two men had worked together and been friends for many years. In 1969 it was Kellogg Foundation Chairman Dr. Mawby who supported the Wege Foundation's first project creating the Center for Environmental Study.

In June, 1991, Wege had returned the favor when Dr. Russell Mawby flew Peter to Costa Rica on the Kellogg plane to meet Dr. Victor Sanchez and see EARTH University. That led to the successful collaboration between Dr. Mawby and Peter Wege to support the environmental university.

In a 2009 news article listing 14 LEED firsts in West Michigan, Peter Wege was named the force behind most of them. The first "green" manufacturing plant was Steelcase, the company founded by his father in 1912; Healthcare, Lack's Cancer Center; the first residence, St. Anthony of Padua rectory; the world's first public LEED built art museum, Grand Rapids Art Museum; and Girl Scout Camp, Anna Behrens.

And Peter was also a major contributor to the first LEED-certified YMCA named for his father's business partner, the David D. Hunting YMCA.

In May 2008, Junior Achievement of the Michigan Great Lakes named Peter Wege winner of the Edward J. Frey Sr. Distinguished Achievement Award recognizing his contributions in education, social services, arts, science, and philanthropy. In 1991 Junior Achievement had also posthumously honored Peter's father Peter Martin Wege, David Hunting, and Walter Idema, founders of Metal Office Furniture Company. These three men behind today's Steelcase were among the first leaders named to Junior Achievement's Business Hall of Fame.

David D. Hunting YMCA

The December issue of *Grand Rapids Magazine* named Peter Wege the first of 25 people considered the city's "most important". Reporter Curt Wozniak credited Peter for making Grand Rapids the greenest-built city for its size in the country. In 2009, Linda Frey, Chairman of the West Michigan chapter U.S. Green Building Council, explained how Peter Wege made that happen.

Linda Frey wrote, "I have the opportunity to work with USGBC representatives from around the country, and I am often asked how conservative Grand Rapids became such a sustainable powerhouse. My answer always includes the leadership of a visionary philanthropist committed to the environment.

"In 2003 Mr. Wege mandated that all capital improvement projects supported by his foundation be LEED certified setting a measurable standard for resource allocation, and giving credibility to the fledgling U.S. Green Building Council and their LEED program."

The USGBC executive went on to say that Wege's announcement "…set the stage for the City of Grand Rapids' prestigious accomplishment of having more LEED buildings per capita than any other city in the United States….Mr. Wege's influence on the architecture of this city goes beyond the number of buildings his foundation has supported. His influence is indirectly felt on every LEED building in West Michigan and the entire nation."

In celebration of Earth Day on April 20, 2008, His Holiness the 14th Dalai Lama of Tibet delivered the Peter M. Wege Lecture on Sustainability at the University of Michigan. Globally admired for his brave stances on human rights and world peace, the Dalai Lama's advocacy for the environment was not as well known. Yet the Buddhist leader called abuse of the environment one of the world's "most serious problems."

CHAPTER THIRTY SIX

WIND FARM AND CAMPUS COLLABORATIONS

"Humanity's goal must be Peace.
The way to Peace is through Education."
Peter M. Wege, Economicology II

In 2008, the U.S. Green Building Council awarded the new Grand Rapids Art Museum a Gold medal making it the greenest museum on the planet. The $75 million, 125,000 square-foot GRAM won LEED points from windows to bike racks. Most remarkable was the fact that housing works of art requires complex air and light conditions, and the GRAM won Gold despite those extra challenges.

In 2012 Steelcase celebrated the company's century in business since its founded as Metal Office Furniture. In honor of the company's history, Steelcase announced another trend-setting leap they'd made into sustainability. The largest office-furniture maker in the world told the media it had reduced its environmental footprint 25 percent as the centerpiece of its 2012 centennial celebrations.

Steelcase leaders were quick to name retired executive Peter Wege as the major force behind the most significant environmental changes they'd made. Redesigning their paint process, for example, reduced their air-polluting volatile organic compounds by 94 percent. That manufacturing change also cut their greenhouse gases by 59 percent, water consumption by 71 percent, and waste by 86 percent.

The March 18, 2008, *New York Times* titled a major business story, "Corporate Sponsorship for a Wind Farm." The corporation was Steelcase, Inc., the company Peter Martin Wege founded in 1912 as Metal Office Furniture. Because Steelcase committed to buying all the renewable energy credits produced by this huge wind farm under construction in Texas, the Grand Rapids corporation had naming rights to the farm.

This opportunity for the office-furniture maker to promote itself as the Steelcase Wind Farm would seem irresistible. Since "green" sells, most corporations couldn't pass that up. But Steelcase did not blink. With a lot to lose in advertising and nothing to gain financially by honoring one low-profile individual, Steelcase chose to pay tribute to the man whose environmental vision had influenced corporate policy for three decades. The eight wind-tower turbines in Panhandle, Texas, were named the Wege Wind Farm.

While Steelcase set the bar as a corporate green citizen with its carbon offsets, a collaboration of major colleges across the country led a similar drive on their college campuses. Not surprisingly, Peter and The Wege Foundation were the moving forces behind academia's push to become carbon neutral.

In 2007, the presidents of several leading colleges and universities formed a coalition dedicated to reducing global warming by making their campuses carbon neutral. The group's name defined its mission: American College & University Presidents' Climate Commitment (ACUPCC). On June 5 and 6 of 2008, The Wege Foundation co-hosted the ACUPCC's second Leadership Summit in Grand Rapids.

In under a year, 550 college and university presidents across the country had pledged to implement energy-efficient practices on their campuses. The fact that Peter Wege was the most significant individual behind this initiative and that his theory of economicology was its driving mission were both acknowledged in the ACUPCC's Summit program:

"More than ten years ago, (Peter) coined the term "economicology" and published his book, ECONOMICOLOGY: the Eleventh Commandment to articulate a vision of a sustainable future based on integrating economic and ecological thinking. The Wege Foundation has long seamlessly supported such thinking through environmental education from kindergarten through post-graduate studies, including endowing the Peter M. Wege Chair of Sustainable Systems at the University of Michigan.

"The Wege Foundation has annually convened the "Economicology group" of 15-20 universities and colleges to share experiences, strategies, and techniques for transforming their institutions, and through them, society at large. The Wege Foundation's support for ACUPCC and this Summit is a natural extension of its Economicology program."

Over two days of meetings and workshops in Grand Rapids, the 150 ACUPCC academic leaders worked on specific ways to improve their schools' sustainability—especially in existing buildings. They deliberated the best ways for integrating sustainability across the curriculum and shared what their schools were doing to educate their own students on global warming.

One of the Summit's featured speakers was Ray C. Anderson, founder of carpet-producing Interface, Inc., and a recognized pioneer in environmental manufacturing. The spokesperson for the academic world was Arizona State University President and ACUPCC Chairman Michael M. Crow.

Among the thank yous to Peter Wege for bringing this collaboration to life was a spontaneous and moving toast from a vice-president of Cape Cod Community College. John Lebica asked the attendees gathered at the closing luncheon to rise and salute Wege saying, "He is somebody who built the strong foundation that the rest of us now can build on."

In the 1990s, Peter Wege's new word "economicology" defined the balance the world must find between "economics" and "ecology." His 1998 book ECONOMICOLOGY: The Eleventh Commandment documents Peter's philosophy that a prosperous world economy requires us to solve environmental problems on a global scale. Thanks to Peter's visionary and philanthropic support, City High/Middle School, the highest-scoring secondary school in the Grand Rapids Public School system, incorporated Wege's world view by offering an International Baccalaureate degree.

Starting with the 2010 school year, City High/Middle 7-10 graders were the first in greater Grand Rapids to have the option of earning an International Baccalaureate degree. Started in Geneva, Switzerland, in 1968, by 2010 this rigorous, two-year curriculum was being taught in over 5,500 schools in 140 countries around the world.

The goal is for the IB diploma to be accepted globally. One requirement is that all students take one of three international languages—Chinese, Spanish, or French. IB's stated mission is to "develop the ability to communicate with and understand people from other countries and cultures."

At the same time he supported the Grand Rapids Public Schools' extensive application for City High/Middle to be named an IB school, Peter was also fulfilling another vision he had for his hometown: a new public school based on economicology.

In 2009 a small group of sixth-grade parents made a leap of faith to sign their children up for a new Economicology School created in a partnership between the Grand Rapids Public Schools and Peter Wege. The first Economicology sixth-graders met at Sigsby School with Peter Wege's two ECONOMICOLOGY books as part of their curriculum. By the next year, the Economicology School had to move into Riverside Elementary because the word was out and the school needed more room.

By 2011, because the program—now called the Center for Economicology (CFE)—had expanded into two classes, the sixth-graders had to move again, this time into larger space at City High/Middle. By 2012, there was a waiting list and the students were matching test scores with GRPS's top performing sixth-grade schools at Blandford Nature Center and the Grand Rapids Zoo.

By the time City High Middle moved into the former Creston High School in 2013, the Center for Economicology was an established program of two sixth-grade classes with 30 students each housed in its own building behind Creston.

Because the natural world is key to their curriculum, the CFE students take frequent outdoor field trips, including visits to wind farms. They also partnered with Grand Rapids' park officials to clean up Riverside Park—one of the field sites where they study invasive species.

The Center For Economicology has now been recognized by the state of Michigan's Rewards program for its outstanding academic success while 40 percent of its students qualify for free/reduced lunches. The national media also picked up on the Center For Economicology when *Parent Magazine* named it one of "the coolest schools in America."

After Peter's death in 2014, retired GRPS principal Dale Hovenkamp, who'd been actively involved setting up the Center for Economicology, shared his memories about Peter.

"What I always appreciated about Mr. Wege was his willingness to give of himself. Before his health started to fail, he would always come to City High/Middle's graduation. He never wanted to make a big deal of it, but would take time to talk with kids and their families after the ceremony. He even asked our students to come and sing at his family holiday party one year at his home. The kids talked about it for weeks."

The same year The Wege Foundation launched the International Baccalaureate degree, it also sponsored a movement to end the sale of plastic water bottles called "Take Back The Tap." Supported by Mayor George Heartwell and the city of Grand Rapids along with Greg Gilmore, owner of the BOB and other area restaurants, the goal was to inform the public that tap water is safer than bottled. City water is more closely monitored than the bottled water taken from the ground by for-profit businesses.

"Take Back The Tap" was written on marine-blue metal water bottles given away during the campaign. The organizers created the acronym CHESS to highlight the five reasons to fill these reusable bottles with tap water instead of buying water in a non-recyclable plastic. Cheaper. Healthier. Earth-friendlier. Safer. Smarter.

CHAPTER THIRTY SEVEN

HONORS, A NEW GRADUATE DEGREE AND SUPER YOOPER

"It's been a wonderful experience and I feel very honored to be able to carry on Peter's and Mark Heckman's legacy in such a positive fashion."

Mark Newman on his Sooper Yooper presentations to young people in Great Lakes schools.

On March 28, 2009, the American Institute of Architects (AIA) named Peter M. Wege its first winner of the David D. Smith Humanitarian Award given by the Grand Valley Chapter of the AIA. The late architect David M. Smith was known for his visionary designs of sustainable school buildings to create optimal learning.

At the awards ceremony, Progressive AE President Bob Daverman asked the auditorium filled with West Michigan architects how many had been professionally influenced by Peter Wege. The show of every single hand made it clear how much the architects had learned from Wege's leadership. They collectively acknowledged that Wege's early advocacy for building according to the U.S. Green Building Council's LEED standards had altered the entire construction landscape in West Michigan.

Daverman went on to say that Grand Rapids' early leap into sustainable building was a direct result of Wege's 2003 decision to fund capital campaigns only if they achieved LEED certification. By 2008, Grand Rapids had put up more LEED square-feet of building based on population than any city in the United States.

Grace Smith, widow of David D. Smith, said when she first learned the AIA was creating this award in her husband's name, "I felt that the award was made for someone as great as Peter Wege."

In thanking Mrs. Smith and the AIA, Wege said he'd planned to be an architect. But during his first year at the University of Michigan, Pearl Harbor was bombed and he signed up immediately. "Instead of architecture school," Wege said, "I ended up flying airplanes for four years during the war."

In April 2010, The Wege Foundation joined The Steelcase Foundation in supporting Catherine's Health Center, a newly expanded medical clinic for the working poor. Named for Catherine McAuley, the 18th Century founder of the Sisters of Mercy, Catherine's provides medical care, screening, and health education for people who earn too much for Medicaid, but whose jobs don't offer health insurance. Funded by both The Wege Foundation and The Steelcase Foundation, the $1.3 million new space in the former Saint Alphonsus grade school earned a LEED Silver designation from the U.S. Green Building Council.

In May 2010, Aquinas College announced a new Master of Sustainable Business degree, the first of its kind in the upper Midwest. At the presenting luncheon, Aquinas President Ed Balog gave Peter M. Wege full credit for this new graduate program that had grown out of a meeting with Wege in 2000. That's when Peter called on the Aquinas faculty for a commitment to preserving the environment.

Aquinas College's Associate Professor of Sustainable Business, Dr. Deborah Steketee, explained the college's new master's degree would combine science, environmental, and business courses. Nancy Hickey, representing Steelcase as a major sponsor of the new degree, said the program fit her company's long-time efforts in green manufacturing and sustainable-business operations.

Hickey explained that Steelcase's experience has proved that their adherence to the triple bottom line—environmental, financial, and social—has given the company a competitive advantage and raised profits.

A highlight of the luncheon was Grand Rapids Area Chamber of Commerce's executive Jeanne Englehart's surprise announcement that the U.S. Chamber of Commerce and Siemens Corporation had just named Grand Rapids the most sustainable midsized city in the nation.

In 2010 Peter Wege and The Wege Foundation made national and international news when The *New York Times* ran a major article featuring the world's first clean-energy art museum recognizing the visionary man behind it, Peter M. Wege.

In 2010, the late environmental artist Mark Heckman, who illustrated Peter Wege's book *ECONOMICOLOGY: The Eleventh Commandment,* won the top Media Great Laker Award during the Great Lakes Restoration Conference in Buffalo, New York, attended by some 300 members from 130 national environmental groups. Heckman was honored for the book *Sooper Yooper* written by his friend Mark Newman and sponsored by Peter Wege and The Wege Foundation.

Using the same colorful artistic technique in *Sooper Yooper* he did for Wege's *ECONOMICOLOGY: The Eleventh Commandment* Heckman's colorful drawings have captivated young readers. The book stars environmental super hero Cooper—a Yooper from Michigan's Upper Peninsula—fighting the invasive species threatening the Great Lakes.

In the fall of 2010, Peter Wege and The Wege Foundation began sponsoring Heckman's friend and collaborating writer Mark Newman to tour Great Lakes schools using *Sooper Yooper* to tell the story. Within five years, the enthusiastic Mark Newman had given his one-hour presentations 1,057 times to 115,000 students in 450 schools in 112 different cities in the five Great Lakes states of Michigan, Illinois, Indiana, Ohio, and Wisconsin.

By 2015 over a dozen schools at different age levels had made Newman's programs a part of their permanent curriculum. Newman's audiences range from elementary to high school students, and he limits the groups to 100 so he can be more interactive.

Mark Newman says of his *Sooper Yooper* outreach to young people, "It's been a wonderful experience and I feel very honored to be able to carry on Peter's and Mark Heckman's legacy in such a positive fashion. The teachers continually offer their gratitude to The Wege Foundation for its willingness to support a multidisciplinary program about the Great Lakes and the environment. It encourages the kids on so many different levels with science, reading, writing, art, etc."

And how else would Peter Wege celebrate his 90th year then by writing a new environmental book, *ECONOMICOLOGY II*. As with his first book in 1998, Wege pulled together the works of environmental experts who have influenced him and who backed up his advocacy for balancing the economy with the ecology.

The writers he quoted run the gamut from his earliest hero John Gardner to contemporary environmentalist Thomas Friedman, and from H.G. Wells to Robert F. Kennedy.

When Joan Kroc, widow of Ray Kroc who founded McDonald's, died in 2004, she left $1.7 billion to the Salvation Army to build 25 first-class family centers in underserved communities around the country. To receive the Kroc grants, the local communities had to raise a matching amount of money. Peter Wege and The Wege Foundation were on board from the get-go to help meet the matching funds and to influence green building.

On October 21, 2010, the Salvation Army opened its $62 million Family Kroc Center at 2500 South Division with a mission of transforming lives through the arts, education, wellness, recreation, and worship. The 99,000-square-foot building on twenty acres gave families in this low-income neighborhood a Disney-like swimming pool, climbing wall, 300-seat auditorium, fitness center, plus education classes from music, to computers, to cooking and nutrition.

But it was underground outside the Kroc where Peter Wege made the greatest difference. Wege convinced the Army to make a daring leap by constructing a geo-thermal heating/cooling system rather than the standard fossil-fuel systems. When word got around that the Kroc's geo-thermal was providing the Kroc's energy, other area builders decided to install the underground pipes too.

One direct result of the geo-thermal was that the Grand Rapids Kroc Center chalked up enough LEED points from the U.S. Green Building Council to earn a Silver medallion.

Kroc Center

CHAPTER THIRTY EIGHT

A SURPRISE TRIBUTE TO A CHERISHED FRIEND

"THAT DAY PETER CHANGED THE
ENTIRE COURSE OF HISTORY FOR GILDA'S CLUB."

GILDA'S CLUB EXECUTIVE DIRECTOR LEANN ARKEMA.

In March 2011 Peter and The Wege Foundation were key players in launching what would become a major March event for West Michigan, LaughFest, to raise money for Gilda's Club. Over 55,000 people attended the first annual, ten-day marathon of comedians entertaining on stages all over the city.

The $330,000 raised that year guaranteed LaughFest was here to stay as a major fundraiser for Gilda's Club and a popular happening for Grand Rapids. And Twink Frey, Deb Bailey, and Susan Smith, three of the cancer survivors who first came up with the idea for a cancer-support center, were laughing along with everyone else during that first LaughFest.

In the fall of 2011, The Wege Foundation participated in the John Ball Park Zoo groundbreaking for $12 million in upgrades. Five million of that, the largest single gift in the zoo's history, came from Bill and Bea Idema. This major improvement expanded the zoo by opening up land that had been unusable because it sat on top of a steep hill.

The solution is now a red funicular that carries zoo guests up to an observation deck, nature trail, and the Bissell Tree House that can be rented for private parties. Not long after completion, area brides found out about the view from the hilltop's expansive Tree House, and, before long, wedding receptions had to be booked long in advance.

The Wege Foundation's 2011 contribution to the zoo was not the first. Because John Ball Park is located on the city's west side, it held special meaning for Peter Wege since it's the neighborhood where his adored mother Sophia Louise Dubridge Wege grew up.

In the early 1980s, Wege had supported the zoo's enhancements of the animals' habitats. Ever protective of the environment and wildlife, Wege was pleased to fund the renovation of exhibits that gave the animals more room and that more closely resembled their natural habitats.

On September 9, 2011, The Wege Foundation staff joined Professor Jonathan Bulkley in Ann Arbor for retirement ceremonies honoring Dr. Bulkley's 43 years with the University of Michigan's School of Natural Resources & Environment. When Dr. Greg Keoleian, Jonathan's partner in the Center for Sustainable Systems, introduced Ellen Satterlee, President of The Wege Foundation, Jonathan knew she was bringing greetings from Peter, who was not well enough to come, but nothing more.

The Bissell Tree House, a popular wedding venue, at the John Ball Park Zoo.

Riding the red funicular up the hill at the zoo to explore the new space for animals, activities, and the Bissell Tree House.

Ellen had to fight tears when she said that Peter and The Wege Foundation were sending more than congratulations. She stunned the full auditorium of Jonathan's family, friends, fans, and students with the news that Peter Wege and The Wege Foundation were establishing the "Jonathan W. Bulkley Collegiate Professorship in Sustainable Systems."

The new award named for Dr. Bulkley will go to a faculty member actively advancing the research and educational mission of SNR & E and the Center for Sustainable Systems (now the School for Environment & Sustainability.) But Peter and The Wege Foundation were not done.

Ellen's second surprise was announcing The Wege Foundation's gift to the University of Michigan of an endowment for students in the dual PhD program between the School of Engineering and the SNR & E.

Peter Wege deeply admired Jonathan Bulkley as a gifted scholar, teacher, and researcher. But beyond that Jonathan was one of Peter's closest friends dating back to the 1991 lunch in Lansing when Wege became the first chair for the University of Michigan's new Prevention Center. That was the beginning of a personal friendship that lasted until the day Peter Wege died.

The month after honoring Dr. Bulkley's retirement in Ann Arbor, Grand Rapid Community College's Foundation declared October 11, 2011, "Peter Wege Night." The GRCC officials called the Grand Rapids native a "local legend and global thinker" as they recognized him for being the third biggest sponsor of GRCC scholarships.

That had all started in 1980 with GRCC Professor Joe Hesse's vision to create scholarships called Teachers of Tomorrow for young people wanting to go into education. Peter liked Hesse's enthusiasm for the cause and, always about education, he liked the cause itself. Teachers of Tomorrow scholarships became reality.

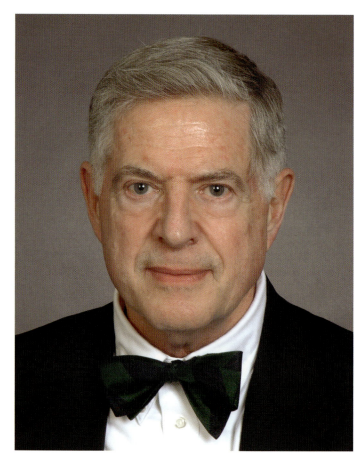

Dr. Jonathan Bulkley

Hesse later said Wege's gift did more than create the scholarships. It opened the door to other benefactors. Once The Wege Foundation's name goes on a project, other donors want to sign on too.

In ceremonies at the Gerald R. Ford Presidential Museum in 2012, Peter M. Wege was elected to the first Michigan Environmental Hall of Fame along with four other leading environmentalists. This new Hall of Fame, created by the Muskegon Environmental Research and Education Society, honors individuals, organizations, and schools in Michigan for environmental stewardship.

In 2017, Peter's good friend, Jack Bails, from the Great Lakes Fishery Trust joined Peter when he was named to the same Hall of Fame.

In April 2012, The Dominican Sisters of Marywood celebrated the expansion and renovation of the Sisters' licensed home for the aged. Originally built in the late 19th Century as the Dominicans' residence, the newly remodeled space is where they now come in their closing years to receive nursing care and rehabilitation services.

The Dominicans partnered with Porter Hills, a long established retirement community, to design three floors meeting differing levels of nursing care. At the dedication, Ellen Satterlee reminded the audience of Peter Wege's lifelong devotion to the Dominicans that began in grade school.

In 2013, after years of planning, a farmer's market for the downtown opened as The Downtown Market. Seven abandoned warehouses were replaced by a soaring structure of recycled wood and concrete crowned by a cathedral glass roof. The $30 million Downtown Market was funded by both private donations, including The Wege Foundation's, and public tax money.

And as with all capital projects The Foundation supports, the Downtown Market applied for LEED certification and earned the highly prized Gold ranking, the first market in the nation to do so. A November 13, 2012, *New York Times* article on the Grand Rapids market commended its location "in a neighborhood of vacant turn-of-the-20th century warehouses… intended by its developers to be a state-of-the-art center of commerce for the culinary arts and fresh local foods."

In May 2013, Ellen Satterlee, President of The Wege Foundation, was awarded an Honorary Doctor of Public Policy degree by Aquinas College. Ellen began working for Peter M. Wege in 1988 as The Wege Foundation's first executive since it started in 1967.

In awarding her the honorary doctorate, Aquinas President Juan Olivarez read from the diploma, "Ellen M. Satterlee's life embodies a commitment to community and service which reflects the mission of Aquinas College and the Dominican charisms." President Olivarez told the audience that "Ellen's lifelong dedication and tireless devotion inspire all those who know her."

In early 2013, The Wege Foundation made two important donations to Clark Retirement Community founded by the Methodist Church. Because Peter's beloved mother Sophia Louise Wege spent her last years in the best nursing home Peter could find, and because he spent so much time visiting her, he knew how important good care meant at the end of life.

The Wege Foundation's first Clark gift went to the benevolent fund that takes care of residents after they can no longer pay. The next gift went to Clark's second campus, Keller on the Lake, for outdoor space called the Shared Garden and Lakeside Pavilion. This second gift gave Clark's residents the opportunity to be refreshed and restored in what Peter referred to as, "God's great gift of Mother Nature." The Shared Garden also weaves into Peter's faith that the mind, body, and spirit are one sacred unity.

In 2014 The Wege Foundation joined with Kendall College of Art and Design launching a contest to solve one of the environment's many "wicked problems," as the rules put it. One reason Peter Wege started the family foundation in 1967 was to deal with the hard reality that mankind was using up Earth's finite natural resources at an unsustainable rate.

And that is the "wicked problem" the Wege Prize challenges students from different colleges and academic disciplines to collaboratively solve. The Wege Prize seeks out innovative ideas toward building a circular, cradle-to-cradle economy. Run by Kendall College, the annual contest reflects Peter Wege's faith in collaborating on new ways to serve both the economy and the ecology.

CHAPTER THIRTY NINE

THE GENEROUS HEART STOPS BEATING… BUT NOT GIVING

"Blessed are those who are attuned to nature's joyous sounds…
Blessed are those who shun war and violence as a solution to our survival."

Peter M. Wege,
Odes From the Heart

After two years in declining health when he could no longer follow his mentor HEW Secretary John Gardner's advice to "Move, Wege, Move," Peter M. Wege died July 7, 2014. The community's overwhelming response left no doubt that he truly had "done all the good he could." Leaders of his favorite causes—from Aquinas to GRAM to the University of Michigan to Mercy Health Saint Mary's—spoke to the profound difference his spirit of generosity had made to their organizations.

But equally telling were the baskets of personal notes delivered to his home from people whose names never get in the newspaper. Each of those handwritten notes of condolence told a story of a small gift from Peter and The Wege Foundation that had made life better for them.

Peter's kindness wasn't always financial. Ellen Satterlee recalls the day she and Peter were late for a meeting at Saint Mary's with other major donors planning to build a state-of-the-art cancer hospital that would become the Richard T. Lacks Cancer. As Ellen tried to hurry Peter along, she saw he was talking to a volunteer driver at the curb who had just escorted his small busload of handicapped passengers into the hospital.

Ellen went back outside to get her boss when she understood. Peter had stopped to tell the man what an important thing he was doing for the people he'd just dropped off. Peter thanked him profusely as he shook the driver's hand—never mentioning that he was the man whose name was on the building they were in front of: The Peter M. Wege Institute for Mind, Body, & Spirit.

Caring for people in need was always one of Peter's driving passions and was behind one of his smaller and less well known charities. In 1990 his friend Elizabeth Crouch came to him with her dream for making college available to special education children. Peter wrote her a $2,000 check on the spot. That figure later went up to $5,000 given every year until he died and is now continued by The Wege Foundation.

Elizabeth's 1990 call on Peter was the beginning of the Noorthoek Academy at Grand Rapids Community College offering classes geared to students who qualify as "educable mentally impaired." Elizabeth's daughter Katie, born with Down Syndrome, was the impetus for this innovative school. Katie's high school friends were going on to college and she wanted to as well.

Twenty-five years later 75 students were enrolled at Noorthoek, named for the late Grand Rapids School Board member James Noorthoek who orchestrated legislation in Michigan that increased support for special education. Noorthoek students spend two hours a week in class and can go as many semesters as they want.

Several students, including Katie, have gone to Noorthoek for over twenty years taking classes in the arts, science, humanities, plus writing poetry for their spring celebration. When Noorthoek students accumulate enough hours to earn an honorary associate's degree, as several have, they graduate in cap and gown along with all the GRCC graduating students.

One year Judge Sarah Smolenski spoke at the spring celebration and invited them to visit her 61st District Court. The next school year Noorthoek's teachers focused the curriculum on the legal system and how it works. By the time they revisited Judge Smolenski's court, the Noorthoek Academy students knew what was going on and why.

Small as this non-profit has been compared to his many seven-figure donations, Noorthoek Academy says a lot about Peter Wege. He loved children and those facing special challenges spoke to his heart. With education always Peter's number-one cause, Katie and Elizabeth Crouch's idea for Noorthoek Academy perfectly fit Peter Wege's vision for "doing all the good" he could.

Peter M. Wege's death did not end his generosity. The board members of three favorite causes were stunned to find out that even after his lifetime of supporting them, he'd gone on to bequeath $1 million to each of them: The Grand Rapids Symphony Orchestra, St. Cecilia Music Center—the oldest art institution in the city, and the Grand Rapids Ballet.

John Varineau, the symphony's Associate Conductor and Peter's close personal friend, explained the posthumous gift from the man he called 'Dad.' "Peter loved to take care of people, nurture their talents and provide exceptional cultural offerings to enhance this community's quality of life," Varineau said. "His love for his hometown and his dedication to local causes has been a big reason for the success of the Grand Rapids Symphony's 85 years."

Cathy Holbrook, Executive Director of St. Cecilia Music Center shared her reaction. "When I got the call about the bequest, I was flabbergasted. Mr. Wege had been a long-time generous supporter of St. Cecilia, but we were not expecting a bequest from him. This is the largest single donation St. Cecilia has received in our 131-years history.

"Everyone at St. Cecilia Music Center is beyond thrilled with this news and we feel so very privileged to be remembered by Mr. Wege in this way. We are so grateful to Mr. Wege and the Wege family." Two years later Wege's gift led the way to a major renovation of St. Cecilia with the large downstairs space christened The Wege Recital Hall.

The Grand Rapids Ballet had long been a favorite cause of Peter M. Wege's, significantly in 2001 when the Meijer-Royce Center for Dance was built with Wege's support. More recently, in 2007, the Grand Rapids Ballet opened its 300-seat Peter Martin Wege Theatre. As was his style, Peter, whose middle name was Melvin, insisted the auditorium be named not for him, but for his father who founded Steelcase.

Glenn Del Vecchio, Executive Director of the Grand Rapids Ballet also went into happy shock when he, too, got a phone call about the $1 million gift. "We've never dealt with this situation before," Del Vecchio said, when asked how the Ballet would use the gift. "We'll put together a plan in the coming months."

Del Vecchio pointed out The Wege Foundation had also contributed $1 million to their $2.5 million debt-retirement campaign and helped recreate Tchaikovsky's *The Nutcracker Suite*. The new version of the Christmas ballet was designed by artist and writer Chris Van Allsburg, a Grand Rapids native who wrote *The Polar Express*. The Van Allsburg *Nutcracker* sold out in its debut the Christmas after Peter died.

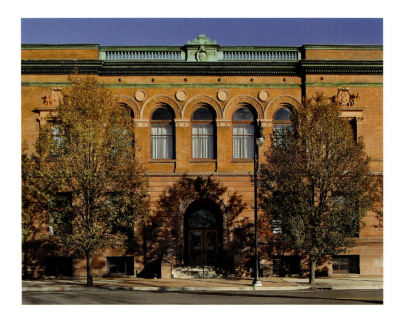

Saint Cecilia Music Center, formerly Saint Cecilia Music Society founded in 1883, is the oldest arts institution in West Michigan. Pictured here is the newly refurbished Royce Auditorium named for the Royce family, long-time supporters of Saint Cecilia. Chuck and Stella Royce were close friends of Peter M. Wege's which is the backstory of Wege's posthumous gift, a major contribution to the Music Center's $2.4 million upgrades.

"His generous donation will contribute to Grand Rapids Ballet's continued growth and further our mission of lifting the human spirit through the art of dance for years to come," Del Vecchio said.

But these three million-dollar gifts were not Peter's only bequests. Another surprised recipient of Peter Wege's estate was John Ball Park Zoo located on the west side near where Peter's beloved mother Sophia Louise Dubridge Wege had grown up.

And after over a half century as recipients of Peter's generosity amounting to $46.5 million, Aquinas College surely didn't expect more. But Peter hadn't forgotten them either. After his death, the school he intended to make the "best Catholic liberal arts college in the country" received a $2.5 million gift from The Wege Foundation.

The donation will create the first economicology collegiate program in the nation "honoring Peter's memory," said Aquinas President Juan Olivarez. President Olivarez always described his friend as Aquinas's "guardian angel". During a period when Aquinas faced serious financial problems, Peter Wege stepped in to make sure the college stayed solvent.

As Olivarez put it, "Peter helped Aquinas grow and prosper in good times and bad times." He spoke about Peter's creating the Sustainable Business program, the first in the country, and now there's a waiting list for students to get in it. "He really made us think about sustainability in new ways."

The Grand Rapids Art Museum covered a wall of its entryway with this eulogy written by Dana Friis-Hansen, Director and CEO of what could have been The Wege Art Museum. "The Grand Rapids Art Museum family mourns the passing of our friend and benefactor, Peter Wege, who has had an enduring impact on us as individuals, as an organization, and as a community.

"Inspired by his parents, Peter's personal mantra was, 'Do all the good you can, for as many people as you can, for all the right reasons.'" This profound yet simple directive steered an extraordinary stream of donations for more than 40 years, both personal gifts from Peter as well as The Wege Foundation…Peter saw his patronage of GRAM as a way to have a meaningful impact in a community he loved. He loved the arts, the earth, and education, and committed his life to improving awareness and innovation in these areas locally, regionally, and nationally."

Dana Friis-Hansen then recounted why GRAM wasn't still in the old Federal Building. In the late 1990s the Art Museum board discussed renovating and expanding the Federal Building where it was housed at the time. Peter Wege had a better idea. GRAM should hire a serious architect to build a modern building in the center of the city and it should be LEED certified with education central to its mission.

As Dana Friis-Hansen put it, "With these three challenges, Mr. Wege forever changed the trajectory of this institution and the arts in Michigan."

Many of GRAM's most treasured works came from Peter's own collection, including Western scenes by Frederick Remington, Alexander Phimister Proctor's bronze "Stalking Panther," and modernist works by Jasper Johns, Ellsworth Kelly, and Robert Rauschenberg.

Peter Melvin Wege 1920-2014

The original Metal Office Furniture plant at 1491 South Division that is now home to the Salvation Army's Adult Rehabilitation Center.

One of the first delivery trucks after Metal Office Furniture was renamed Steelcase in 1954.

What better way to end this story than in Peter's own reflection written near the end of his life. No one could summarize Peter M. Wege's heart better than his own three closing paragraphs.

"I am proud of my German heritage and the fact that our family name Wege means way in German. In German a Wegbereiter is one who goes ahead—a pioneer. My grandfather Conrad Wege was the first in his family to leave Germany for the United States. My father Peter Martin Wege led the way into the new industry of manufacturing steel office furniture. I have tried to follow their legacy by lighting the "Wege" to a sustainable environment.

"My grandfather couldn't speak English when he made his Wege to the United States. My father went into debt borrowing $75,000 so he could lead the Wege into the brand new world of metal office furniture. I have invested the best of my time, energy, and assets into The Wege Foundation so we could lead the Wege toward saving our planet, raising the level of intelligence, and enhancing health through holistic medicine

"Do all the good you can, in all the ways you can, to all the people you can, just as long as you can. This quote from my book *ECONOMICOLOGY: The Eleventh Commandment* summarizes the philosophy of The Wege Foundation since I started it in 1969. We have tried to chart the way toward a better future for all people by: conserving the environment, raising educational standards—both public and secular; and providing quality mind-body-spirit health care."

Construction of the original Metal Office Furniture factory in 1912 on a $75,000 bank loan to Peter Martin Wege.

PRAYER FOR COMPASSION AND UNDERSTANDING

Oh, Lord, God—
We pray that you will address our human weaknesses and
give us the strength to understand our frailties.
What are we doing to the life-support system you gave us,
the clean air, clean water of a healthy existence?

We have fouled our life-support system by human ignorance
and the pursuit of personal achievements and unreliable goals,
which cause human greed instead of need.

Give us compassion and understanding of why we are here on
this dot in the Universe. We have lost touch with you, Lord,
and beg that you bring us back to the realization that we need
to grow a healthy mind, body, and spirit in your name. AMEN.

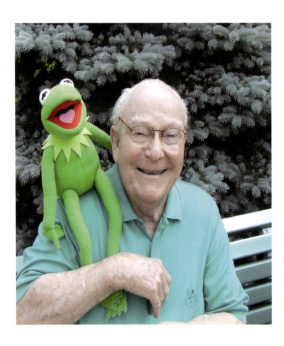

Peter M. Wege:
February 19, 1920 – July 7, 2014

AFTERWORD

Then-CEO Ellen Satterlee commissioned this history of The Wege Foundation for publication on its 50th anniversary. But, it is also a very personal book. It's impossible to describe the Foundation without portraying its founder, Peter Wege, for whom philanthropy was personal.

Susan Lovell's meticulous research compiles many moving stories of friendships and experiences that animated Wege's giving. It roots his generosity in his love for his parents, his commitment to his hometown community, his belief that a healthy environment and vibrant economy go together, and his sense of responsibility for sharing his good fortune with fellow residents. Writing a history of The Wege Foundation necessarily requires telling personal stories about Peter. But, this is not a biography. At the risk of hagiography, by design this book's focus is Peter Wege as philanthropist. It paints a partial picture of a complex man.

This is also a personal book because Susan and her husband, Ray, became close friends with Peter over the years it describes. She witnessed firsthand many of the acts of generosity depicted. She knows many of the key individuals whose passions Peter shared, who guided his giving and who, in turn, became Peter's friends. Writing this book has been an act of love for Susan.

Now the challenge for The Wege Foundation is to translate Mr. Wege's generous spirit, commitment to West Michigan and relationship-driven giving into sustained and effective grantmaking. Fortunately, the Foundation has a board of directors led by his descendants that is dedicated to meeting this challenge and to continuing to "do all the good it can for as many as it can" in perpetuity.

In this, the story of The Wege Foundation and of Peter Wege continues.

Mark Van Putten
President and CEO
The Wege Foundation

August 2017

ACKNOWLEDGEMENTS

We know a picture's worth a thousand words, and my deepest thanks to these good people who provided the wonderful photographs that make this book come to life.

Carl Apple
Sister Colleen Ann
Beth Brown
Dave Bulkowski
Terry Dixon
Maureen Donnelly
Michael Erickson
Luke Ferris
Kate Flores
Dr. Winnie Hallwachs
Jennifer Hudson
Helaine Hunscher
Keri Kujala
Jill Maslowsky
BriAnne McKee
Greg Meyer
Sister Mary Paul Moller
Kyle Pray
Father Mark Przybysz
Kathy Reagan
Julie Ridenour
Kim Ritz
Ryan Ruppert
Leslie Schoen
Amy Snow-Buckner
Roger Snyder
Denny Sturtevant
Cindy Vanderberg
Katie Van Doeselaar
Jim Visser
Kendra Gunter Willis
Megan Zars

INDEX

A

Abundant Life Ministries, 121
Adams, Celeste, 80
Adams, John, 38
Adult Rehabilitation Center (ARC), Salvation Army's, 135–136
affordable housing, in Heartside neighborhood, 52, 54
Aigner, Dennis, 105
air quality, Wege's concern for, 41
Alksnis, Greg, 17
Alten, Mathias, 74
Ameen, David, 69
American Cancer Society, 27, 28, 32, 72
American College & University Presidents' Climate Commitment (ACUPCC)., 150
American Defense ribbon, 24
American Institute of Architects (AIA), 152
Amway Grand Plaza hotel, 52
Anderson, Ray C., 150
Ann, Sister, 43–44
Anna Behrens Camp, 107, 145
Aquinas College, 17, 29–30, 32, 45, 46, 60, 62–63, 90–92, 93, 118, 152, 164
"Aquinas Grows" funding drive, 62
Aquinas Performing Arts Center, 74, 92
Área de Conservación Guanacaste (ACG), 85
Arias, Oscar, 47, 83
Arkema, Leann, 97
Armstrong, Neil, 38
Arts Council Art Award, 80

B

Babcock, Bishop Allen James, 29, 32
Babies Welfare Guild, 83
Bailey, Deb, 97, 155
Bails, Jack, 101, 158
Baldwin, Ralph, 41
Balkan Relays, 24
Balog, Ed, 152
Barnes, Jack, 41
Baxter Christian School, 130
Baxter Community Center, 130–131
Beaton, James H., 38
Becker, Dick, 24, 130
Beelen, Melanie, 130
Beldon Foundation, 122
Bierbaum, Rosina, 90
Biffo the Environmental Clown, 38
Bissell Tree House, 82, 155, 157
Blandford Environmental Education Program, 113
Blandford Nature Center, 113–114, 117, 139, 151
Blandford Schools, 112, 113–114, 117
Bleke, Bert, 110, 113, 117
Bliss, Rosalynn, 63
Blodgett Hospital, 28, 48
Blythefield Country Club, 17
board of directors, Wege on, 25
Book Tower, 81
Bowman, Harold E., 38, 71
Boy Scouts of America, 30, 32, 45, 107
Bravo Awards, 77
Bren School, 105
Brennan, Michael, 60
Brown, Norman, 86
Brown Military Academy, 20
Bruntland, Gro Harlem, 90
Buchsbaum, Andy, 127
Bukowski, Arthur F., 32
Bulkley, Jonathan, 88, 89, 105, 155, 158
Bulkowski, Dave, 64
Butterworth Hospital, 28, 48, 140
Byron Center Hospital, 71

C

C.A. Frost Environmental Science Academy, 96, 139
Calder, Alexander, 74
Calder Plaza, 74
Calkins, Dick, 47
Camp Ann Behrens, 45
Camp Blodgett, 83
Camp O'Malley,, 119
Cape Eleuthera Island School, 138
Carson, Ben, 137
Carson, Rachel, 29
Cascade Engineering, 107
Cascade Hills Country Club, 22
Catherine's Health Center, 152
Catholic Central High School, 52, 92
Catholic Junior College, 62. *see also* Aquinas College
Catholic Secondary Schools, 52, 54, 55–56
Center for Economicology (CFE), 151
Center for Environmental Study, 27, 37–39, 40–41, 46–47, 74, 83
Center for Sustainable Systems, 89
Chamberlain, Wallace M., 38
Charles Stuart Mott Foundation, 64, 122
Chase Township Public Library, 108–109
Chernobyl meltdown, 46
Chi Psi Fraternity, 21
Chuck Roast fundraiser, 60
City Commission, 134

City High/Middle School, 107, 150–151
Clark Retirement Community, 159
Clean Air and Clean Water Act, 129
Clugston, Rick, 137
Clune, Dottie, 67
Coleman, Mary Sue, 143
Collins, Francis S., 144
Community Media Center, 67
Community Sustainability Partnership, 134
Cook, Peter, 38, 59, 75
Cook Foundation, 114
Costa Rica, conservation efforts in, 47, 83–85, 86–87
Cotter, Gilbert, 51
Council of Michigan Foundations, 92
Creston High School, 151
Crouch, Elizabeth, 160–161
Crouch, Katie, 161
Crow, Michael M., 150

D

Dalai Lama, 148
Daley, Richard, 127, 128
Damien Marie, Sister, 44
Dana Building, 105, 143
Daniels, Jeff, 145
Daverman, Bob, 152
David D. Smith Humanitarian Award, 152
Davis, Albert F., 29
de Paul, Sister Vincent, 23, 93
Degage' Ministries, 52
Del Vecchio, Glen, 161, 164
DeVos Performing Arts Center, 74
Disability Advocates, 63–64
Divine Diva's Salon, 67
Divine Grace Church, 136, 137
Dockery, Mary Jane, 113
Dodge, Kay, 47
Dolan, Harry, 118, 118–119
Dominican Sisters of Marywood, 158–159
Donald Bren School of Environmental Science & Management, 105
Doty-Nation, Pam, 142
Dougherty, Ken, 21
Downtown Development Authority, 134
Downtown Market, The, 159
DuBos, Rene, 46
Dubridge, Eugene, 19
Dubridge, Gerard, 19
Dubridge, Sophia. *see* Wege (Dubridge), Sophia
Durfee Building, 106

Dwelling Place, 52, 54, 55–57, 58, 66–67, 136
Dyer-Ives Foundation, 67, 134

E

Earth Charter, 137
Earth Day, 39, 137
EARTH University, 86–87, 145
East Grand Rapids City Complex, 46
Eastern Avenue Christian Reformed Church, 130
Economicology, 26, 29, 46, 150, 153
economicology, theory of, 40–41, 64, 88, 90–91, 103, 105, 107, 132, 141–142, 150, 164
ECONOMICOLOGY meeting, 137
Economicology School, 151
Edward and Susan Blodgett Lowe estate. *see* Holmdene estate
Edward J. Frey Sr. Distinguished Achievement Award, 145
Ehlers, Vernon, 126–128
Emanuel, Rahm, 128
Emeritus Award, Aquinas College, 93
Englehart, Jeanne, 153
Ervine, Christine, 105, 140
Ettawageshik, Frank, 127
Ettesvold, Winfred, 38
European Theatre medal, 24
Exhibitor's Building, 38, 45

F

Faith in Motion, 63–64, 136
Father Flanagan's Boy's Town, 26
Federal Building, 164
Ferguson Hospital, 48, 136
Field Army American Cancer Society, 23
First of America Bank, 54
Fischer, George, 41
Flanagan, David, 132–133
Flanagan, Kathleen, 132
Flanagan, Lloyd, 132–133
Ford, Dick, 40
Ford, Ellen, 40
Ford, Gerald, 40, 43, 62
Ford, William Clay, 90
Foster Parents for War Children, 26
Franciscan nuns, in Lowell, Michigan, 42–44, 47
Franciscan Rhythms, 43
Frank Doran, M.D., Distinguished Service Award, 71
Frankforter, Weldon D., 38
Frey, Linda, 148
Frey Foundation, 59, 122, 134
Friends of Transit, 63–64

Friis-Hansen, Dana, 164
Fuller, Buckminster, 27

G

Gardner, John, 37–39, 42, 69, 129
General Fireproofing, 18
Gerald R. Ford Presidential Museum, 158
Gietzen, Georgia Woodrick, 144
Gilda's Club, 26, 97, 155
Gillett, Richard, 38
Gilmore, Greg, 151
Girl Scouts of America, 45, 107, 145
God's Kitchen, 55, 57
"Good Samaritan" campaign, 28
Goodall, Jane, 23
Goodrich building, 57
Gore, Al, 90
Grand Bank, 60
Grand Ideas Garden, 134
Grand Rapids Art Museum, 27, 74–75, 139, 145, 149, 164
Grand Rapids Ballet, 74, 80, 161
Grand Rapids Children's Museum, 80, 144
Grand Rapids Circle Theatre, 92
Grand Rapids Civic Theater, 80
Grand Rapids Community College, 47, 67, 141, 158, 160
Grand Rapids Community Foundation, 54, 59, 114, 132, 134
Grand Rapids Fire Department, 119, 140
Grand Rapids Historical Commission, 56–57
Grand Rapids Historical Preservation Commission, 71
Grand Rapids Jaycees Family Park., 50
Grand Rapids Public Education Fund, 50
Grand Rapids Public Schools, 110, 113, 117, 121, 139, 150
Grand Rapids Symphony, 74, 77, 78–79, 161
Grand Rapids University, 62
Grand Rapids Urban League, 45, 50
Grand Rapids Zoo, 151
Grand River cleanup, 101
Grand Valley Council of Boy Scouts, 45, 107
Granholm, Jennifer, 145
Great Depression, 19
Great Lakes Collaboration Implementation Act, 126
Great Lakes Fishery Trust, 101, 103, 158
Great Lakes Water Resources Compact, 128
Green Grand Rapids, 134
Greeson, Alyce, 144

H

Haan, Paul, 134
Habitat for Humanity, 106, 140–142

Hackett, Jim, 121
Hall of Fame, Aquinas College, 92
Hallwachs, Winnie, 47, 83, 85
Hanna, Jack, 96
Harmon, Tom, 21
Harvard Leadership Change Group, 110, 113
Hauenstein, Ralph, 71, 92
Hauenstein Neuroscience Center, 71
Haviland, J. Bernard, 38
Healing Our Waters, 122–128
Healing Our Waters-Great Lakes (HOW-GL) Coalition, 127–128
"Heart of the Matter" campaign, 59
Heart of West Michigan United Way, 60
Heartside Grocery, 54, 57
Heartside Ministry, 58–60
Heartside neighborhood, 8, 14, 52–54, 56, 56–57, 58–60
Heartwell, George, 58, 60, 134, 151
Heckman, Mark, 46, 64, 153
Heffron, Clayton, 133
Heffron, Mary Lou, 133
Henry, Frederick, 22
Henry, Victoria. see Wege (Henry), Victoria
Henson-Conant, Deborah, 78
Herkimer Hotel, 55–57
Hershey dam removal, 101, 103
Hesse, Joe, 158
Heysteck Auditorium, 60
Hickey, Nancy, 153
Highlands Golf Course, 114
Hills, Porter, 159
Hoexum, Ken, 54
Hoffius, Leonard, 38
Holbrook, Cathy, 161
Holmdene estate, 62
Hooker, David, 81
Hope Lodge, American Cancer Center's, 72
Hoskins, Kenny, 136–137
Hovenkamp, Dale, 151
Hruby, Norbert J., 38
Hunting, David D., 19, 36, 38, 145
Huntington Bank, 67

I

Idema, Bea, 155
Idema, Bill, 155
Idema, Henry, 121, 145
Idema, Walter, 19
Institute for Mind, Body, and Spirit, 69
Interdenominational Ministerial Alliance, 136–137

Interface, Inc., 150
Interlochen, 80
International Baccalaureate degree, GRPS and, 150–151
Invention & Alchemy, 79

J
Jacobson's Store, 121
Janzen, Dan, 47, 83, 85
Jarecki, Clare F., 90
Jarecki Center, at Aquinas College, 46
Jarecki School for Advanced Learning, 90–91
javelin throwing, 20–21
Jenson, Dylana, 78
J.L. & J.M. Cornell Company, 18
John Ball Zoo, 82, 92, 155, *156*, 164
John Collins Park, 30
John P. Varineau Outstanding Music Education Award, 79
John XXIII, Pope, 29
Johns, Jasper, 164
Johnson, Diane, 107–109
Johnson, Tristan, 48
Jonathan W. Bulkley Collegiate Professorship in Sustainable Systems, 158
Jordan College, 46
JR's Deli, 67
Junior Achievement of the Michigan Great Lakes, 145

K
Kathleen Battle Gala, 78
Keller on the Lake, 159
Kellogg, Will K., 27
Kelly, Ellsworth, 164
Ken and Judy Betz family, 114
Kendall Colllege of Art and Design, 159
Kennedy, Robert F., Jr., 91–92, 129, *131*
Kent County Medical Society, 28
Kent County TB Society, 27
Keoleian, Greg, 88, 89, 105, 155
Kermit the Frog, 38, 105
Kiel, Herman, 17
Kiernan, Tom, 126, 127
Kirk, Mark, 127
Kresge Challenge grant, 130–131
Kress, Duane, *36*, 38
Kretschmer Hall, 92
Kroc, Joan, 154
Kuyper College, 62

L
La Grande Vitesse, 74
Lacks, Mary Jane Morrissey, 70
Lacks, Richard J., 70
Lacks Cancer Center, 70, 71, 145
Ladd, Everett L., 38
LaGrand, Melissa, 67
Lake Forest Academy, 20
Lake Michigan Academy, 60
Lakeside Pavilion, 159
Land Conservancy of West Michigan, 95, 114, 134
Land Use Stewardship Award, 133
Laugh Fest, 155
Leadership in Energy and Environmental Design (LEED), 70, 71, 73, 75, 105, 106, 113, 130, 140–142, 145, 148, 149, 152, 154, 159, 164
League of Women Voters, The, 42
Learning Center, 67
Learning Corner, 67
Lebica, John, 150
Lee, Kaiulani, 29
Lenox Building, 54, 55–57
Leonard, Sister Mary, 17, 23, 93
Levin, Carl, 128
Life Process Center, 44
Little Sisters of the Poor, 26
Liz's House, 57
Lockington, David, 78
Lorina's, 67
Lowell, Michigan, Franciscan nuns in, 42–44, 47
Lynch, Richard, 38

M
MacDonald, Jon, 74
Make the Impossible Possible, 121
Malthus, Thomas, 26
Margaret, Sister Mary, 43
Marietta Safe Cabinet Company, 18
Mary Jane Dockeray Visitor Center, 114
Maryknoll Fathers, 26
Master of Sustainable Business degree, Aquinas College, 152–153
Mawby, Russell, 86, 145
Maxey, Chris, 138
Maywood Academy, 42
McAuley, Catherine, 152
McAuley Building, 56–57
McCarthy, Terri, 47, 137
McClurg, Barb, 67
McCorkle, Philip, 69, 71, 73
McDonough, William, 89

McHarg, Ian, 41
McInerney, William K., 38
McKay, Jim, 97
McKay, Twink Frey, 97, 155
Meijer, Fred, 80, 81, 82
Meijer, Lena, 80, 81, 82
Meijer Gardens, 81
Meijer-Royce Center for Dance, 161
Mercy Health Lacks Cancer Center, 71. *see also* Lacks Cancer Center
Metal Office Furniture, 14–16, 19, 20, 25, 33, 135, 149
Meyer, Greg, 21
Michigan Colleges Foundation, 32, 45
Michigan Community Blood Center, 48
Michigan Hall of Fame, 158
Michigan Heart Center, 82
Michigan Trails Girl Scouts, 45, 107
Millenium Park, 21
mobile MRI donation, 48
Morris, Carla, 144
"Ms. Melanie's Sparrows," 131
Muller, James, 136
Munkenbeck & Marshall, 76
Muscular Dystrophy Association, 27
"Music for Life" campaign, 77
Muskegon Environmental Research and Education Society, 158
Muskegon River Watershed Assembly, 101, 103

N

National Parks and Conservation Association, 122
National Pollution Prevention Center for Higher Education., 88, 89. *see also* Center for Sustainable Systems
National Resources Defense Council, 122
National Wildlife Federation, 27, 96, 122
National World War II Memorial, 24
Natural Wildlife Federation, 23
Nature Conservancy, 95
Nauta, Gay, 133
Nauta, Vern, 133
Neal, Teresa Weatherall, 110
Nelson, Paul, 90, 93
Neuman, Frank, 38
Newby, Patricia, 121
Newman, Frank, 28
Newman, Mark, 153
Newman, Peter, 90
Noorthoek, James, 160
Noorthoek Academy, 160–161
North Africa, Peter Wege in, 22–23

Northern Great Lakes Forest Project, 95
Notre Dame Retreat House, 26
nuclear power, Wege's concern about, 46
Nunn, Phillip, 36

O

O'Keefe, Donald, 30
Old Kent Bank Building, 38
Olivarez, Juan, 67, 159, 164
O'Malley, Frank, 119
Opening Doors campaign, 130
Opera Grand Rapids, 74
Osteopathic Hospital, 48
Our Hope, 42
Outdoor Discovery Center, 119
Outstanding Service Award, Aquinas Alumni Association, Outstanding Service Award., 93
overpopulation, Wege's interest in, 25–26, 38–39

P

Palm, Lorena, 107
Palmer, Boris, 38
Paola, Eric S., 85
Parnell Avenue Corridor, 134
Pastine Vaudette. *see* Wealthy Theater
Patricia, Sister, 42–43
Pedden, John, 38
Pekich, Barb, 58, 59
Peninsular Club, 75
Peter M. Wege Chair of Sustainable Systems, 89
Peter M. Wege Guest House, 72
Peter M. Wege Institute. *see* Institute for Mind, Body, and Spirit
Peter M. Wege Lectures, 90, 143, 148
Peter M. Wege Library, 81
Peter M. Wege Pro Am Tournament, 17
Peter Martin Wege Scholarship, 18
Peter Martin Wege Theatre, 80, 161
Peter M.Wege Environmental Education Center, 114
Pew, Robert C., 38
Planned Parenthood, 42
Polio Foundation, 27
Pollack, Lana, 103
Porphyrogenes peterwegei, 85
Prevention Center, University of Michigan, 158
Proctor, Alexander Phimister, 164
profit sharing, at Metal Office Furniture, 16
Prothro, Winston B., 38
Przybysz, Father Mark, 93, 105, 106–107, 114
Purchase of Development Rights program, 132–134

R

Racial Justice Institute, 121
Radner, Gilda, 97
Raushenberg, Robert, 164
Reading Garden, 109
Reeds Lake, 30–31
Reflections Award, 92
Reformed Bible College, 62
Remington, Frederick, 164
Renihan, Joseph, 38
Rhodes Rib Crib, 67
Richard J. Lacks Cancer Center, 56–57, 160Ridenour, Rich, 78
Rita, Mother Superior, 42
Riverkeepers movement, 92, 129
Riverside Elementary School, 151
Roberts, David, 75
Rockford and Byron Center, 110
Rockford Construction, 106
Rosa Park Circle, 75
Rosenzweig, Leonard, 38
Royce, Chuck, 79–80
Royce, Stella, 79–80
Royce Auditorium, *162*
Russell G. Mawby Award, 145

S

Sacred Heart, 62. *see also* Aquinas College
Saint Mary's Hospital, 160
Salvation Army, 135–136, 154
San Diego Army and Navy Academy, 19
Sanchez, Victor, 86–87, 145
Sanderson, James, 38
Sandmann's, 67
Satterlee, Ellen, 47, 50–51, 52, 56, 58, 89, 97, 107, 130–131, 135, 155, 159, 160
Satterlee, Gale, 50
Sax, Joseph, 90
scapular medal, Peter Wege's, 23
School of Natural Resources and the Environment (SNRE), 87–88, 105, 143, 155
Schweiger, Larry J., 40, 128
Screenbeater Silk Screen, 67
Seamon, Dave, 52, 56
Secchia, Joan, 117
Sense of Wonder, 29
Seymour, Steve, 24
Shared Garden, 159
SHOWtime! 2001, 67
Sierra Club, gifts to, 27
Silent Observer, 118

Silent Spring, 29
Silver Line, 64
Simpson, Allen, 75
Sisters of Mercy, 42
Smith, Grace, 152
Smith, Susan, 97, 155
Sojourners Transitional Living Center, 48
solar power, Wege's interest in, 46
Sooper Yooper, 153
Sophia's House, 73
South Division apartment, 8, 52–53
South East Economic Development (SEED), 65
St. Alphonsus grade school, 152
St. Andrews Church, 8
St. Anthony's church, 22, 94, 106, 145
St. Anthony's School, 106, 114
St. Cecilia Music Center, 74, 79, 161, *162*
St. Francis Award, 131
St. John's Home, 29
St. John's Orphan Asylum, 26, 29
St. Lazarus Retreat House, 32
St. Mary's Hospital, 28–29, 32, 42, 48, 52, 56, 69–70
St. Stephen's church, 17, 26, 93, 93–94
St. Stephen's grade school, 17, 70, 93–94
Stair, Ella, 17
Steelcase, Incorporated, 14, 16, 24, 25, 31, 33, 40–41, 47, 50, 54, 55, 59, 74, 78, 88, 89, 129, 145, 149, 152–153
Steelcase Foundation, 152
Steelcase Windfarm, 149
Steinman, Annoesjka, 113
Steketee, Deborah, 153
Stockton, Edward, 36, 38
Stoddard, Chuck, 60
Stoddard, Jan, 60
Strategy For A Livable Environment, A, 37, 38, 42, 129
Strickland, Bill, 121
Student Advancement Foundation, 117
Sturtevant, Denny, 52, 54, 55–57, 66–67, 71, 136
Summers, Tom, 91
Sustainable Business program, Aquinas College, 164

T

Taft, Robert, 127
Take Back the Tap initiative, 151
Tassell Michigan Technical Education Center, 141
Teachers of Tomorrow scholarships, 158
Tourangeau, Melia, 77, 79
Transitions program, 48
Turning Point (Salvation Army), 135–136
Tutu, Desmond, 92

U

Umana, Alvaro, 47, 83
Umezu, General Yoshijiro, 23
Union of Concerned Scientists, 122
United Fund, 32
United Growth for Kent County, 133–134
United States Green Building Council, 41, 70, 73, 75, 80, 105, 106, 130, 140, 143, 148, 149, 152, 154
University of California, Santa Barbara, environmental building at, 46, 105
University of Michigan, 20, 45, 89, 89–90, 105, 143–144, 148, 155, 158
U.S. Public Interest Research Group, 122
USDA Farm Protection program, 133

V

Van Allsburg, Chris, 161
Van Putten, Mark, 122
Varineau, John, 78–79, 161
Varneau, Gordy, 19, 38, 65
Varneau, Lillian, 19, 65
Varneau, Oscar, 19, 65
Vaughn, Henry, 38
Verhey Carpets, 67
"Victor" waste basket, 21
Vierson III, Neil, 36
Villa Verde, 106, 114
Vocational Skills Center, Grand Rapids, 45
Voinovich, George, 128
Von Domelen, Peter, 33

W

W. K. Kellogg Foundation, 27–28, 37, 86, 145
Waite, George, 141
Walsh, Joseph, 38
Warm, David, 38
Wealthy Bakery, 67
Wealthy Street Business Alliance, 67
Wealthy Street business district, revitalization of, 65
Wealthy Theater, 19, 65–67
Wealthy-Division neighborhood. see Heartside neighborhood
Wege (Dubridge), Sophia, 14, 17, 19–20, 26, 73, 83, 94, 155, 159, 164
Wege (Henry), Victoria, 22, 28
Wege, Christopher Henry, 27, 28, 29
Wege, Conrad, 167
Wege, Diana, 28
Wege, Johanna, 28
Wege, Jonathan Michael, 31, 42
Wege, Mary Gretchen, 24
Wege, Peter Martin, 14–15, 17, 18, 19–20, 21, 23, 31, 33, 62, 72, 81, 135, 145, 167
Wege, Peter Martin II, 45
Wege, Peter Melvin. *see also* Wege Foundation
   American College & University Presidents' Climate Commitment (ACUPCC). and, 150
   Aquinas College donations and, 32, 62–63, 90–92, 164
   Aquinas College Master of Sustainable Business degree and, 152–153
   Aquinas College student center and, 32
   Baxter Community Center and, 130–131
   beginnings as community leader, 28–30
   Blandford Schools and Blandford Nature Center, 113–114, 117
   C.A. Frost Environmental Science Academy and, 96, 139
   Camp Blodgett donation and, 83
   Center for Economicology (CFE) and, 151
   Center for Environmental Study and, 27, 37–39, 40–41, 46–47, 74, 83
   Chase Township Public Library and, 108–109
   childhood companions of, 19
   Costa Rica conservation efforts of, 47, 83–85, 86–87
   David D. Smith Humanitarian Award and, 152
   death of, 160–161
   Disability Advocates and, 63–64
   Divine Grace Church and, 137
   Dominican Sisters of Marywood and, 158–159
   Downtown Market and, 159
   early grants of, 17–18
   early life, 14–15
   ECONOMICOLOGY meeting and, 137–138
   Edward J. Frey Sr. Distinguished Achievement Award and, 145
   Ellen Satterlee and, 50–51
   Emeritus Award to, 93
   environmentalism of, 22–24, 25–26, 27, 29–31, 32, 37–39, 40–41, 45–47, 83–85, 86–88, 89–92, 95–96, 101–105, 106–109, 122–128, 129, 132–134, 137–138, 149–151, 159
   establishment of Wege Foundation, 16, 32
   farm preservation and, 132–134
   Father Mark Przybysz and, 93–94, 106–107
   Gilda's Club and, 26, 97
   Gordy Varneau and, 19
   Grand Rapids Art Museum and, 27, 74–75, 139, 145, 149
   Grand Rapids Community College and, 158, 160
   Grand Rapids Fire Department and, 119, 140
   Grand Rapids Magazine's "25 Most Important" and, 148
   Grand Rapids Police Department and, 118–119
   Grand Rapids Public Schools and, 110, 113, 117, 139, 150–151
   Habitat for Humanity and, 140–142
   healthcare-related donations of, 48–51

Heartside ministry and, 58–60
Heartside neighborhood revitalization and, 52–54, 56–57, 58–60
honorary doctorate (University of Michigan), 143–144
Interdenominational Ministerial Alliance and, 136–137
John Ball Zoo donations and, 82, 92, 155, 164
at Lake Forest Academy, 20
Laugh Fest and, 155
Lenox Building sale and, 55–57
Meijer Gardens and, 81
Michigan Hall of Fame and, 158
Michigan Heart Center donation and, 82
at military school, 19–20
Muskegon River Watershed Assembly and, 101, 103
Nature Conservancy and, 95–96
Noorthoek Academy and, 160–161
patron of the arts, 27, 74–77, 78–80, 161
posthumous donations of, 161, 164
in post-WWII 1940s, 25
in post-WWII 1950s, 25–28
racial profiling and, 119–120
Robert F. Kennedy Jr. and, 91–92, 129
Russell G. Mawby Award and, 145
Salvation Army and, 135–136
Salvation Army Kroc grants and, 154
School of Natural Resources and the Environment (SNRE) and, 87–88, 89, 105, 143
Sooper Yooper outreach and, 153
St. Mary's Hospital gifts of, 69–73
Take Back the Tap initiative and, 151
University of Michigan and, 20–21, 144, 158
Wealthy Street Business district revitalization and, 65–67
Wege Speakers Series and, 90–92
Wege Wind Farm and, 150
Wege's parents as inspiration for, 14–16
West Michigan Center for Arts and Technology and, 121
Wittenbach-Wege Environmental Center and, 95
women's issues and, 42–44
during World War II, 21, 22–24
Wege Center for Sustainable Fisheries, 138
Wege Foundation
    American College & University Presidents' Climate Commitment (ACUPCC) and, 150
    Aquinas College and, 45, 62–63
    Área de Conservación Guanacaste (ACG) conservation and, 85
    Blandford Nature Center and, 113
    Blandford School and, 113–114
    Center for Environmental Study and, 27, 36, 41, 46–47, 82
    Chase Township Public Library and, 108
    Clark Retirement Community and, 159
    Disability Advocates and, 64
    Donald Bren School of Environmental Science & Management and, 105
    Downtown Market and, 159
    EARTH University and, 86–87
    Ellen Satterlee joins, 50–51
    farm preservation and, 132–134
    Grand Civic Theater and, 80
    Grand Rapids Art Museum and, 74–77, 164
    Grand Rapids Ballet and, 80
    Grand Rapids Children's Museum and, 144
    Grand Rapids Public Schools and, 107, 113
    Grand Rapids Symphony and, 78–79
    Grand Rapids Urban League and, 45
    Grand River cleanup and, 101
    Grand Valley Council of Boy Scouts and, 45
    Great Lakes Fishery Trust and, 101
    Habitat for Humanity and, 140–141
    Healing Our Waters and, 122
    Heartside neighborhood revitalization and, 14, 54–55, 60
    John Ball Zoo and, 82, 155
    Jonathan W. Bulkley Collegiate Professorship in Sustainable Systems and, 158
    Jordan College and, 46
    Kendall Colllege of Art and Design and, 159
    Laugh Fest and, 155
    Meijer Gardens and, 81
    Michigan College's Foundation and, 45
    National Wildlife Federation and, 96
    Noorthoek Academy and, 160–161
    Outdoor Discovery Center and, 119
    Peter M. Wege Guest House and, 73
    Richard J. Lacks Cancer Center and, 56
    St. John's Home and, 29
    St. Mary's Hospital and, 73
    Student Advancement Foundation and, 117
    Tassell Michigan Technical Education Center and, 141
    Transitions program and, 48
    Turning Point (Salvation Army) and, 136
    University of Michigan and, 45, 105
    Vocational Skills Center and, 45
    Wealthy Business District revitalization and, 66–67
    Western Michigan Center for Arts and Technology and, 121
    Women's Resource Center and, 42
Wege Institute for Mind, Body, and Spirit, 29
Wege Nature Trail, 81
Wege Prize, 159
Wege Recital Hall, 161

Wege Speakers Series, 90–92
Wege Wind Farm, 149
Weimer, Hans, 43
Weir, Sandy, 140
Welch, Jim, 121
Wells, George, 22
Wells, Maurie, 22
Wells, Pamela, 139
Wepman's Pawn Shop, 54, 55
West Catholic High School, 92
West Michigan Center for Arts and Technology, 121
West Michigan Environmental Action Council, 41
West Michigan Environmental Action Council (WMEAC), 46
Whole Foods, 87
wHY Architecture, 76
Wilcox, Marsha, 133
Wilderness Society, The, 122
Williams, Theodore C., 38
Williams College, 46
Wills, Kendra, 134
Wittenbach-Wege Environmental Center, 95, 110
Wolters, Kate Pew, 63
Women's Committee of the Grand Rapids Symphony, 42
women's issues, Wege's concern for, 42–44
Women's Resource Center, 42
Woodrick, Aleicia, 144
Wozniak, Curt, 148
WWII Victory medal, 24

Y
Yantrasast, Kulapat ., 76
YMCA, 50
"Young, Gifted and Black" program, 78

Z
Zaglu, Jose A., 86
Zondervan Publishing, 51